AF693594

Table of Contents

1 **The Genesis of Virtual Worlds** 5
1.1 Defining Virtual Reality 8
1.2 A Brief History of VR 12
1.3 The Building Blocks of VR 16
1.4 Hardware: Gateways to Immersion 19
1.5 Software: The Soul of VR 23

2 **Asynchronous Interactions** 27
2.1 Multiplayer VR Experiences 31
2.2 The Challenge of Real-Time 34
2.3 Asynchronous Solutions 38

3 **Crafting Immersive Narratives** 43
3.1 Storytelling in Virtual Reality 46
3.2 Interactive Narratives 49
3.3 The Role of the User 53
3.4 Emotional Engagement in VR 57
3.5 Future of VR Storytelling 60

4 **The Symphony of Code** 65
4.1 Game Engines and VR 69
4.2 Physics Engines: Simulating Reality 73
4.3 Networking: Connecting Virtual Worlds 76

5 **Designing Virtual Environments** 81
5.1 3D Modeling for VR 85

5.2 Level Design and User Experience 89
5.3 Optimizing Performance in VR 92
5.4 Creating Believable Worlds 96
5.5 Accessibility in VR Design 99

6 The Future of Virtual Reality 105
6.1 Emerging Technologies in VR 108
6.2 The Metaverse and its Implications 112
6.3 Ethical Considerations in VR 115

7 VR Beyond Entertainment 121
7.1 VR in Education and Training 124
7.2 Therapeutic Applications of VR 128
7.3 VR for Business and Industry 132
7.4 The Expanding Horizon of VR 136
7.5 Virtual Reality and Society 140

1 The Genesis of Virtual Worlds

The journey into virtual reality begins long before the donning of a headset. It starts with a fundamental question: what is virtual reality? At its core, VR is an immersive, interactive, computer-generated simulation of a three-dimensional environment. This simulated reality can mimic the real world or transport us to fantastical realms, limited only by the bounds of imagination and computational power. The crucial element is the sense of presence, the feeling of actually being within the digital environment, a sensation crafted through a combination of sensory input and interactive feedback. This feeling of presence distinguishes VR from other media, transforming it from passive observation to active participation. This immersion fosters a sense of agency, allowing users to interact with the virtual world and influencing their own experiences within it.

The concept of virtual reality is not new. Its roots can be traced back to panoramic paintings and stereoscopic viewers of the 19th century, creating an illusion of depth and immersion. These early attempts, while rudimentary, planted the seeds for the technological advancements that would follow. The mid-20th century saw the development of the Sensorama, a mechanical device that attempted to simulate a motorcycle ride through multiple sensory inputs, including visuals, sound, vibration, and even smell. While technologically impressive for its time, it was cumbersome and impractical. The first true head-mounted display (HMD), the "Sword of Damocles," was developed in the 1960s, offering users a glimpse into a simple, wireframe 3D world. Although primitive by today's standards, it represented a significant leap towards realizing the dream of true virtual immersion. The following decades saw further experimentation and refinement, laying the groundwork for the consumer VR experiences we see today.

The realization of immersive virtual reality relies on a complex interplay of hardware and software components, each playing a critical role in the creation and experience of virtual worlds. The most recognizable hardware component is the HMD, the gateway to the virtual world. Modern HMDs use sophisticated displays, lenses, and sensors to create stereoscopic images, tracking head movements with precision to provide a believable sense of spatial awareness. These displays refresh at high frame rates to minimize latency and motion blur, crucial for maintaining the illusion of presence and preventing motion sickness. Beyond the HMD, input devices like hand controllers and haptic suits provide the means to interact with the virtual environment, translating real-world movements into virtual actions. Specialized treadmills and omnidirectional platforms further enhance immersion by allowing users to walk and move freely within the virtual space.

While hardware provides the physical interface, software is the soul of the virtual reality experience. At the heart of most VR applications lies the game engine, a complex piece of software that acts as the foundation for creating and managing the virtual world. The engine handles rendering, physics, audio, and user input, orchestrating these elements into a cohesive and interactive experience. Within the engine, specialized systems work tirelessly behind the scenes. Physics engines simulate realistic interactions between objects, ensuring that virtual objects behave according to the laws of physics. Rendering engines transform 3D models and environments into the visual images displayed on the HMD, employing advanced techniques like ray tracing and global illumination to create visually stunning and believable virtual worlds. Audio engines create immersive soundscapes, adding another layer of realism and depth to the experience. Networking solutions enable multiple users to share the same virtual space, opening up possibilities for collaborative and social VR experiences. This intricate interplay of hardware and software forms the foundation upon which compelling and immersive virtual experiences are built, blurring the lines between the physical and the digital.

1.1 Defining Virtual Reality

Immersiveness, often touted as the defining characteristic of virtual reality (VR), goes beyond mere visual fidelity. It's the feeling of truly being somewhere else, of inhabiting a different space. This sense of presence, of existing within a virtual environment, is achieved through a complex interplay of sensory inputs, primarily visual and auditory, working together to convince your brain that the artificial world is real. Consider how your perception shifts when wearing noise-canceling headphones: the world outside fades, and your focus sharpens on the immediate soundscape. VR takes this concept further, enveloping you in a synthesized reality designed to elicit a sense of place. The success of this illusion relies heavily on how effectively the technology can mimic real-world sensory experiences.

The visual component of VR is largely delivered through head-mounted displays (HMDs). These devices, worn like goggles, house screens for each eye, creating stereoscopic images that simulate depth and perspective. High refresh rates and low latency are crucial for minimizing motion sickness and maintaining the illusion of reality. Imagine the jarring effect of a delayed image when turning your head – the disconnect would instantly shatter the immersive experience. Advanced HMDs also incorporate eye-tracking technology, allowing for foveated rendering. This technique renders the area you're directly looking at in high detail, while peripheral areas are displayed at lower resolution, optimizing processing power and enhancing visual realism.

Auditory cues play a vital role in creating a believable virtual world. Spatial audio, which mimics how sound travels in the real world, adds another layer of immersion. Imagine hearing a virtual dog bark behind you, and instinctively turning your head to locate the source. This accurate sound placement reinforces the feeling of actually being present in the virtual environment. Just as with visuals, low latency in audio delivery is critical. A lag between your actions and the corresponding sounds would break the illusion and diminish the sense of presence. High-quality audio, including realistic environmental sounds and directional cues, contributes significantly to the overall VR experience.

Beyond sight and sound, haptic feedback contributes to the sense of touch within a virtual world. This can range from the simple vibrations of a controller, simulating the recoil of a virtual gun, to more complex systems involving gloves or full-body suits that provide pressure and temperature sensations. Imagine feeling the texture of a virtual object or the resistance of a virtual surface. These tactile experiences further blur the lines between the real and virtual worlds, deepening the sense of immersion. While still in its early stages, haptic technology is rapidly evolving, promising even more realistic and nuanced tactile feedback in the future.

Interaction within the virtual environment is key to a compelling VR experience. Traditional controllers, while functional, often lack the nuance and intuitiveness of real-world interactions. Imagine trying to pick up a virtual object with a standard gamepad – the lack of fine motor control can be frustrating. More advanced input methods, such as hand tracking and gesture recognition, offer greater freedom and naturalism. The ability to reach out and manipulate virtual objects with your bare hands adds a level of immersion that traditional controllers simply can't match.

The applications of VR extend far beyond gaming and entertainment. In healthcare, VR is used for surgical training, pain management, and physical therapy. Imagine a surgeon practicing a complex procedure in a safe, virtual environment, honing their skills without risk to a patient. In education, VR can transport students to ancient civilizations, the depths of the ocean, or the surface of Mars, offering immersive learning experiences that traditional textbooks simply can't replicate. This ability to experience different environments and scenarios firsthand can revolutionize how we learn and interact with the world around us.

Different types of VR experiences cater to various needs and levels of immersion. Mobile VR, using a smartphone inserted into a headset, offers an accessible entry point, but with limited tracking and graphical capabilities. Standalone VR headsets, which don't require a PC or phone, provide a more immersive experience with improved tracking and processing power. High-end PC VR systems offer the most realistic and immersive experiences, but require a powerful computer and often come with a higher price tag. Choosing the right system depends on your individual needs and budget.

The evolution of VR technology continues at a rapid pace. Researchers are exploring new ways to enhance immersion, including improved display technologies, more sophisticated haptic feedback systems, and even brain-computer interfaces. Imagine a future where virtual experiences are indistinguishable from reality, where we can seamlessly interact with virtual worlds using only our thoughts. While such advancements may seem like science fiction, they represent the potential of VR to fundamentally transform how we interact with digital information and experience the world around us.

The ethical implications of increasingly immersive VR experiences warrant careful consideration. Issues of privacy, data security, and the potential for addiction are important considerations as this technology becomes more widespread. Imagine a scenario where virtual experiences become so compelling that they begin to replace real-world interactions and relationships. As VR continues to evolve, it's crucial to address these ethical challenges proactively, ensuring that this powerful technology is used responsibly and for the benefit of humanity.

Developing content for VR requires a unique set of skills and considerations. Traditional game development techniques often don't translate directly to the immersive world of VR. Developers need to consider factors like user comfort, motion sickness, and the unique challenges of designing for a 360-degree environment. Imagine designing a virtual world that feels natural and intuitive to navigate, while also minimizing the risk of motion sickness. As the VR industry continues to grow, the demand for skilled VR developers will only increase.

1.2 A Brief History of VR

The Sensorama, a bulky mechanical marvel dreamt up in the mid-1950s, offered a glimpse into a future where we could experience simulated realities. It engaged multiple senses – sight, sound, smell, even vibration – but remained a curious prototype, too complex and costly for mass production. This early attempt, while ultimately unsuccessful commercially, laid a crucial foundation by highlighting the desire and potential for immersive experiences. It seeded the idea that technology could transport us to other worlds.

The 1960s witnessed the birth of the Headsight, a contraption considered by many to be the first actual head-mounted display (HMD). Unlike the Sensorama, its purpose was more practical, aimed at military applications like remote bomb disposal. It offered a rudimentary form of virtual reality, relaying video feed to a user wearing a headset. This marked a significant shift towards individual, wearable displays, a concept that would become central to VR development. While still crude by today's standards, the Headsight demonstrated the feasibility of creating a visually immersive experience through a head-mounted device.

The following decade saw the rise of computer graphics, paving the way for more believable virtual environments. Researchers at the University of

Utah began developing complex 3D modeling techniques. This advancement was crucial, as it allowed for the creation of digital spaces that could be interacted with, rather than simply viewed. This era also saw the emergence of the first data glove, allowing users to manipulate virtual objects, further enhancing the sense of immersion. These developments, though often confined to academic and research settings, provided the building blocks for future consumer-grade VR systems.

Atari, a pioneer in the early video game industry, explored VR technology in the early 1980s. However, the limitations of computing power at the time hindered their ambitions. The arcade-style experiences they envisioned demanded far more processing power than available technology could provide. Consequently, the resulting prototypes were simplistic and underwhelming, far from the immersive worlds imagined by developers. The failure of Atari's early VR ventures highlighted a crucial challenge: realizing the full potential of virtual reality would require significant advancements in computing technology.

The term "virtual reality" itself was popularized in the late 1980s by Jaron Lanier, founder of VPL Research. His company developed specialized VR equipment, including gloves and headsets, targeted towards professional applications. These devices, though expensive and still relatively primitive, sparked renewed interest in the field. Lanier's work brought virtual reality into the public consciousness, establishing a framework for how we understand and discuss the technology today.

The 1990s saw the first tentative steps towards consumer-grade VR. Sega, Nintendo, and other gaming companies introduced VR gaming consoles. However, these systems were plagued by technical issues, often causing motion sickness and providing a less-than-convincing immersive experience. The high price point and underwhelming performance led to commercial failure, effectively halting the mainstream adoption of VR for over a decade. This period became a cautionary tale, demonstrating that consumer expectations for VR were high, and that delivering on those expectations required significant technological leaps.

The 21st century ushered in a resurgence of interest in VR. Driven by advancements in computer processing power, graphics cards, and display technology, a new generation of VR headsets emerged. Companies like Oculus Rift, HTC, and Sony began developing high-quality, consumer-friendly VR devices. These headsets offered improved resolution, wider fields of view, and more accurate tracking, leading to significantly more immersive experiences. The renewed interest in VR extended beyond gaming, with applications emerging in fields such as healthcare, education, and engineering.

The past few years have witnessed the continued evolution of VR technology. Standalone headsets, untethered to PCs or consoles, have gained popularity, increasing accessibility and ease of use. Improved tracking and haptic feedback devices have further enhanced immersion, allowing for more realistic interactions with virtual environments. The development of advanced hand tracking systems has eliminated the need for handheld controllers in some applications, creating a more natural and intuitive user experience.

Looking towards the future, the trajectory of VR appears promising. Ongoing research and development efforts focus on enhancing realism, resolution, and comfort. The integration of eye-tracking technology promises to optimize rendering and improve user interfaces. Furthermore, advancements in areas like augmented reality (AR) and mixed reality (MR) are blurring the lines between the physical and digital worlds, creating new possibilities for immersive experiences. The convergence of these technologies suggests a future where the boundaries between real and virtual will become increasingly fluid.

The development of VR has been a long and iterative process, marked by both promising breakthroughs and disappointing setbacks. From the clunky mechanical contraptions of the mid-20th century to the sleek, high-tech headsets of today, the journey of virtual reality reflects a persistent human desire to explore beyond the confines of the physical world. As technology continues to advance, the potential applications of VR seem limitless, promising to reshape how we interact with each other, learn, work, and experience the world around us. The history of VR is not simply a chronicle of technological development; it's a testament to the enduring power of human imagination and our relentless pursuit of immersive experiences.

1.3 The Building Blocks of VR

Immersive experiences don't just magically appear. They are carefully constructed, layer by layer, using fundamental building blocks. Understanding these components is crucial for anyone venturing into the world of virtual reality. It's like learning the alphabet before writing a novel – essential for crafting compelling and believable virtual worlds.

The first, and perhaps most obvious, building block is the visual aspect. This encompasses everything the user sees: the environment, the objects within it, and even the avatars of other users. Creating believable visuals requires a deep understanding of 3D modeling, texture mapping, and lighting techniques. Think of a simple wooden crate in a virtual room. The model defines its shape, the texture gives it the appearance of wood grain, and the lighting determines how it looks under different light sources. These elements work together to create the illusion of a real object. Getting these details right is crucial for immersion; a poorly textured object or unrealistic lighting can instantly shatter the sense of presence.

Sound design is another critical component, often overlooked. While visuals capture our attention, sound truly immerses us in a virtual environment. Imagine walking through a virtual forest: the rustling of leaves, the chirping of birds, the distant howl of a wolf. These sounds create a rich tapestry of auditory information that enhances the sense of place. Furthermore, spatial audio, which simulates how sounds travel in the real world, adds another layer of realism. This allows users to pinpoint the source of a sound, creating a more believable and interactive experience. Without carefully crafted sound design, even the most visually stunning virtual world can feel flat and lifeless.

Next, we have user interaction, the bridge between the user and the virtual world. This includes how users navigate the environment, manipulate objects, and interact with other users. Intuitive controls are paramount. Imagine trying to pick up a virtual object with clunky, unresponsive controls; the experience would be frustrating and immersion-breaking. Effective interaction design should feel natural and seamless, allowing users to effortlessly engage with the virtual world. This might involve using motion controllers to mimic hand movements or employing eye-tracking technology to allow users to select objects with their gaze.

Haptic feedback adds another dimension to the experience. This refers to the sense of touch in the virtual world. Imagine feeling the rumble of an engine as you grip a virtual steering wheel or the subtle resistance of a virtual button as you press it. These tactile sensations significantly enhance immersion, making the virtual world feel more tangible and real. While not always essential, haptic feedback can add a powerful layer of realism to virtual experiences, particularly in simulations and gaming.

Beyond these core elements, there are more nuanced building blocks that contribute to the overall experience. Consider the narrative structure of the virtual experience. Just like a good story, a compelling VR experience needs a beginning, middle, and end. This narrative arc can guide the user through the virtual world, providing context and motivation for their actions. A well-crafted narrative can transform a simple virtual tour into an engaging and memorable experience.

Performance optimization is another crucial, albeit less glamorous, building block. A virtual world can be visually stunning and feature intricate interactions, but if it runs poorly, the experience will be ruined. Lag, stuttering, and long loading times can quickly break immersion. Therefore, optimizing the performance of the VR application is essential for a smooth and enjoyable experience. This involves careful management of resources, efficient coding practices, and thorough testing on the target hardware.

User interface (UI) and user experience (UX) design also play a critical role. The UI encompasses all the elements that allow the user to interact with the application, such as menus, buttons, and other controls. The UX, on the other hand, refers to the overall experience the user has while interacting with the application. A well-designed UI/UX should be intuitive, easy to use, and visually appealing, allowing users to seamlessly navigate the virtual world and access its features without frustration.

Finally, consider the social aspects of VR, particularly in multi-user environments. The ability to interact with other users in a shared virtual space adds a whole new dimension to the experience. This requires careful consideration of avatar representation, communication systems, and social etiquette within the virtual world. Designing effective social interactions can transform a solitary VR experience into a vibrant and engaging social gathering.

Building compelling virtual reality experiences requires a deep understanding of these fundamental building blocks. By carefully considering each element and how they interact, developers can create immersive and engaging virtual worlds that transport users to another reality. Remember, the success of a VR experience hinges not just on cutting-edge technology but also on a thoughtful and well-executed design. Each element, from the visual details to the sound design to the user interface, plays a crucial role in crafting a truly immersive and unforgettable experience.

1.4 Hardware: Gateways to Immersion

The tangible components of your virtual reality setup are more than just pieces of technology; they are the portals through which you step into other worlds. Understanding their nuances and how they interact is crucial for a truly immersive experience. Don't just settle for the defaults. Explore, tweak, and optimize to find what resonates with your individual needs and preferences. This journey into virtual reality is personal, and your hardware should reflect that.

Headsets are your window to the virtual world. Resolution dictates the clarity of the visuals, impacting the sense of presence. A higher resolution means a sharper, more detailed image, reducing the "screen door effect" where you perceive the spaces between pixels. Refresh rate, measured in Hertz (Hz), determines how smoothly the image updates. A higher refresh rate minimizes motion blur and contributes to a more comfortable experience, especially during fast-paced action. Field of view (FOV) affects how much of the virtual world you can see at once. A wider FOV provides a more immersive perspective, closer to natural human vision. Consider these factors carefully when choosing a headset, balancing cost with desired performance.

Beyond the visual display, tracking is paramount. Accurate tracking translates your real-world movements into the virtual environment seamlessly. Inside-out tracking utilizes cameras on the headset itself to map your surroundings and determine your position, offering a convenient setup without external sensors. Outside-in tracking relies on external sensors or base stations to track the headset and controllers, often providing greater precision and a larger play space. Each method has its strengths and weaknesses, so consider your available space and desired play style.

Controllers are your virtual hands, allowing you to interact with the environment and objects. Haptic feedback, the vibrations and resistance they provide, adds another layer of immersion by simulating the feeling of touch. Ergonomics are also crucial for comfortable extended use. Some controllers prioritize intuitive button layouts, while others offer more advanced features like finger tracking for finer control and gestures. Explore different controller types to find the best fit for your preferences and the specific VR experiences you enjoy.

Audio plays a surprisingly significant role in virtual reality immersion. Spatial audio simulates the way sound behaves in the real world, allowing you to pinpoint the direction of sounds and enhancing the sense of presence. Headphones are generally recommended for the best audio experience, though some headsets offer integrated speakers. Consider factors like sound quality, comfort, and noise isolation when selecting your audio setup. A high-quality audio experience can dramatically enrich your immersion.

Your computer is the engine that powers your virtual reality experiences. A powerful graphics card (GPU) is essential for rendering complex virtual environments and maintaining a smooth frame rate. The processor (CPU) handles the game logic and other computations, and sufficient RAM ensures smooth performance. Check the recommended specifications for your chosen VR headset and games, and aim to exceed them if possible. A well-equipped computer is a foundation for a truly immersive VR experience.

Cables, while often overlooked, can significantly impact your VR experience. A long, high-quality cable allows for freedom of movement without signal loss or interference. Wireless adapters can eliminate the cable entirely, providing even greater freedom, but may introduce latency or require additional setup. Consider your play space and preferences when choosing your connection method. A clean and organized cable management system can also enhance your overall VR setup.

Beyond the core components, accessories can further enhance your VR experience. Tracking pucks can be attached to your feet or other body parts for full-body tracking, adding another layer of immersion and realism. Haptic vests provide tactile feedback to your torso, simulating impacts and other sensations. Specialized gloves allow for more nuanced hand interactions and finger tracking. Explore these accessories to further customize your VR experience.

Setting up your physical play space is just as important as choosing the right hardware. Ensure you have adequate space free from obstacles to move around safely. Consider the lighting in your room, as excessive light can interfere with tracking. Establish boundaries within your play space to avoid collisions with real-world objects. A well-designed play space can significantly improve your comfort and safety while using VR.

Calibration is crucial for ensuring accurate tracking and a comfortable experience. Follow the manufacturer's instructions carefully to calibrate your headset, controllers, and any other tracking devices. This process typically involves defining your play space and establishing the relationship between your real-world movements and the virtual environment. Proper calibration is essential for a seamless and immersive VR experience.

Maintaining your hardware is key to ensuring its longevity and optimal performance. Clean your headset lenses regularly with a microfiber cloth to remove smudges and dust. Keep your controllers clean and free of debris. Store your equipment properly when not in use to protect it from damage. Regular maintenance will help ensure your VR setup continues to provide immersive experiences for years to come. By understanding and optimizing each component of your hardware, you open the door to truly immersive virtual reality experiences.

1.5 Software: The Soul of VR

The magic of Virtual Reality doesn't reside in sleek headsets or hand controllers. It lives in the code, the algorithms, the intricate software that breathes life into these digital worlds. Without robust software, VR is just a clunky helmet displaying a static image. Software is the soul, the invisible force orchestrating every interaction, every sensation, every breathtaking vista in the virtual realm. This isn't just about creating pretty pictures; it's about building believable experiences.

Understanding the software ecosystem is crucial for anyone venturing into VR development, even at a beginner's level. We're talking about the game engines, the SDKs (Software Development Kits), the APIs (Application Programming Interfaces), and the myriad tools that form the foundation of any VR experience. These tools are your brushes, your chisels, your musical instruments – they empower you to sculpt, shape, and compose your own realities. Think of a game engine like Unity or Unreal Engine as the bedrock upon which you build. They provide the physics engine, the rendering pipeline, and a host of other functionalities that handle the complex calculations required for immersive VR. Imagine trying to calculate the trajectory of a thrown object in VR, accounting for gravity, air resistance, and collisions, all in real-time. The game engine does this heavy lifting for you, allowing you to focus on the creative aspects.

SDKs, on the other hand, are like specialized toolkits tailored to specific hardware. For instance, the Oculus SDK provides the tools and libraries needed to interact with Oculus headsets, while the SteamVR SDK does the same for Valve Index and other compatible devices. These SDKs bridge the gap between your software and the hardware, ensuring seamless communication and optimal performance. APIs act as messengers, allowing different software components to talk to each other. Imagine you want to integrate hand tracking into your VR experience. The hand-tracking API provides a standardized way for your software to access and interpret data from the hand-tracking sensors. This modularity allows developers to leverage existing functionalities without reinventing the wheel.

Choosing the right software tools is a pivotal decision, influencing the scope, complexity, and ultimately, the success of your VR project. Consider the target platform. Are you developing for mobile VR, standalone headsets, or PC-based VR? Each platform has its own strengths and limitations, requiring specific SDKs and optimization strategies. Mobile VR prioritizes performance efficiency due to limited processing power, whereas PC-based VR can handle more graphically intensive experiences. Factor in your project's specific needs. If you're building a simple 360-degree video player, a lightweight SDK might suffice. However, a complex interactive simulation demands a robust game engine and a suite of specialized APIs. Beyond the core tools, a vast ecosystem of supplementary software plays a vital role in VR development. 3D modeling software like Blender or Maya is essential for creating the assets that populate your virtual world. Audio design tools, such as Audacity or Pro Tools, allow you to craft immersive soundscapes that enhance the sense of presence. Think about spatial audio, which simulates the way sound travels in the real world, adding another layer of realism to the experience. Specialized software for haptic feedback design can further enhance immersion by adding tactile sensations to virtual interactions.

Mastering the interplay between these different software components is the key to crafting truly captivating VR experiences. This involves not just technical proficiency, but also a deep understanding of user experience principles. Consider factors like comfort, accessibility, and intuitive interaction design. VR sickness, caused by discrepancies between visual and vestibular cues, can quickly break immersion. Careful optimization and thoughtful design are crucial to minimize this issue. Accessibility considerations ensure that your VR experience is inclusive and enjoyable for users with diverse abilities. Intuitive interaction design allows users to navigate and interact with the virtual world naturally and effortlessly.

The software development process is an iterative journey of experimentation, refinement, and constant learning. Start small, experiment with different tools, and gradually expand your skillset. Don't be afraid to embrace the learning curve. The VR landscape is constantly evolving, with new tools and technologies emerging at a rapid pace. Staying curious and adaptable is essential for navigating this dynamic environment. Join online communities, attend workshops, and explore open-source projects to connect with fellow developers and stay abreast of the latest advancements.

The world of VR software is a vast and exciting frontier, ripe with possibilities. With the right tools and a spirit of exploration, you can create experiences that transcend the boundaries of the physical world and transport users to realms of pure imagination. Remember, the software is not merely a means to an end; it's the very essence of the VR experience, the invisible hand that shapes our perceptions and emotions within these digital realms. So, dive in, explore, and let your creativity run wild. The future of VR is waiting to be written, one line of code at a time.

2 Asynchronous Interactions

Persistence in virtual worlds introduces a compelling dimension to user interaction. Consider a collaborative art project within a virtual environment. One user might sculpt a form, save their progress, and log off. Later, another user enters the same virtual space and adds texture to the sculpture, building upon the previous user's contribution. This asynchronous collaboration allows for creative expression without requiring simultaneous presence, accommodating diverse schedules and geographical locations. This opens a world of possibilities for artists across the globe to contribute to a single piece, each adding their own unique style and perspective over time. This asynchronous approach transforms the creative process into a layered dialogue, evolving organically with each contribution.

Asynchronous interactions can also facilitate unique gameplay mechanics. Imagine a treasure hunt within a vast virtual landscape. One player might discover a clue and leave a virtual note for others to find. Days later, another player stumbles upon this clue, continuing the hunt. This form of asynchronous gameplay creates a sense of shared discovery and fosters a community around the virtual world, even without direct interaction. This sense of shared purpose and persistent progress fosters a deeper connection to the virtual world and its inhabitants. The world feels alive and responsive, even in the absence of other players.

Beyond collaborative creation and gameplay, asynchronous interactions can enhance narrative experiences in VR. Imagine a virtual museum where visitors can leave virtual comments on exhibits. These comments, visible to future visitors, create a layered narrative around the artifacts, reflecting diverse perspectives and interpretations. A user from Japan could share their cultural understanding of an ancient artifact, while a user from Egypt might provide historical context. This asynchronous dialogue enriches the museum experience, transforming it from a passive observation into an active, evolving narrative.

The implementation of asynchronous interactions requires careful consideration of data management and synchronization. Changes made by one user need to be reliably saved and reflected for other users when they enter the virtual environment. This necessitates robust server infrastructure and efficient data handling techniques. Version control systems, similar to those used in software development, can be employed to track changes and resolve potential conflicts. Imagine, for instance, two users simultaneously editing different parts of a virtual building. A version control system could seamlessly merge their changes, preventing data loss and ensuring consistency.

Furthermore, designing user interfaces for asynchronous interaction presents unique challenges. How can we effectively communicate the presence and activities of other users who are not currently online? Visual cues, such as timestamps on objects or virtual avatars representing offline users, can provide context and a sense of continuity. Imagine seeing a faint outline of another user's avatar, indicating where they last interacted within the environment. This provides a subtle yet powerful connection to the asynchronous community inhabiting the virtual space.

Moreover, asynchronous interactions can facilitate personalized experiences within shared virtual environments. User preferences and progress can be saved and loaded, allowing for customized experiences each time a user enters the virtual world. Imagine a virtual library where your reading progress is saved, bookmarks are persistent, and personalized recommendations appear based on your previous selections. This level of personalization enhances immersion and fosters a sense of ownership within the shared virtual space.

Consider the implications for virtual education. Students could collaborate on projects within a virtual classroom, contributing asynchronously to shared presentations and simulations. Teachers could provide feedback and guidance through annotated virtual objects, creating a dynamic and personalized learning experience. This asynchronous approach to education transcends geographical barriers and allows for flexible learning schedules, catering to diverse learning styles and needs.

In the realm of virtual tourism, asynchronous interactions can enhance the sense of discovery and exploration. Imagine visiting a virtual recreation of ancient Rome. You could leave virtual notes on landmarks, sharing your observations and insights with other virtual tourists. Later, you might discover comments left by previous visitors, adding layers of historical context and personal anecdotes to your experience. This asynchronous exchange transforms the virtual tour into a collaborative exploration, enriching the sense of place and connection to the past.

Asynchronous interactions also open doors for innovative social experiences in VR. Imagine a virtual park where users can leave messages on a virtual bulletin board, organizing meetups or sharing recommendations for virtual activities. This asynchronous communication fosters a sense of community and encourages social interaction within the virtual space, even without requiring simultaneous presence. This fosters a vibrant and dynamic social ecosystem within the virtual world.

Finally, consider the potential for asynchronous storytelling in VR. Imagine a virtual world where users can contribute to an evolving narrative by leaving virtual objects or recording audio logs. These contributions become part of the ongoing story, shaping the virtual world and influencing the experiences of future visitors. This form of collaborative storytelling empowers users to become active participants in the narrative, blurring the lines between creator and consumer. The virtual world becomes a living document, a testament to the collective imagination of its inhabitants.

2.1 Multiplayer VR Experiences

Stepping into a shared virtual world with others adds a whole new dimension to the immersive experience. The social interaction, the collaborative possibilities, and the shared sense of presence create a unique form of entertainment and connection. Navigating these spaces effectively, however, requires understanding a few key elements.

Comfort is paramount. Before diving into a bustling multiplayer VR environment, take the time to fine-tune your headset's fit. Adjust the straps, ensure the weight is evenly distributed, and position the lenses for optimal clarity. A comfortable setup will allow you to fully engage with the virtual world without distractions. This is especially crucial in fast-paced games or experiences requiring extended periods in VR. A poorly fitted headset can quickly lead to discomfort and detract from the overall enjoyment.

Once you're physically comfortable, consider your virtual representation. Your avatar is your extension in the digital realm, a visual representation of yourself. Experiment with different customization options to create an avatar that reflects your personality and preferences. Whether it's a stylized representation or a realistic depiction, your avatar is how others perceive you in the shared space. This sense of personal expression contributes to the immersive quality of multiplayer VR.

Effective communication is crucial for a positive multiplayer experience. Many VR platforms offer built-in voice communication, allowing you to talk to other players in real-time. Take the time to familiarize yourself with the controls and adjust microphone settings for optimal clarity. Clear communication enhances teamwork, facilitates social interaction, and contributes to a more immersive and engaging experience. Nonverbal communication, through gestures and avatar movements, also plays a significant role. Be mindful of your virtual body language.

Navigating social interactions in VR requires a degree of awareness and etiquette. Treat others with respect, just as you would in the real world. Be mindful of personal space and avoid disruptive behavior. Remember that behind every avatar is a real person. Positive interactions foster a welcoming and enjoyable environment for everyone. Building a positive reputation within a VR community can lead to more rewarding experiences and connections.

Exploring different genres of multiplayer VR experiences can broaden your horizons. From collaborative puzzle-solving adventures to competitive esports arenas, the possibilities are vast. Consider your interests and preferences when choosing which experiences to try. Experimenting with different genres will help you discover the types of VR interactions that resonate with you most. Each genre offers unique challenges and opportunities for social interaction.

Multiplayer VR games often involve teamwork and coordination. Communicate effectively with your team, share information, and work together towards common goals. Understanding the strengths and weaknesses of your team members can enhance your collective performance. Supporting each other and celebrating successes fosters a positive team dynamic and increases the likelihood of achieving shared objectives. In cooperative experiences, teamwork is often the key to overcoming challenges.

Competition in VR can be exhilarating, but maintaining a sportsmanlike attitude is essential. Respect your opponents, acknowledge their skills, and avoid gloating or belittling behavior. Winning is not everything; the true reward lies in the shared experience and the connections forged through competition. A positive and respectful approach to competition fosters a healthy and enjoyable environment for all participants. Embrace the challenge and focus on improving your own skills, rather than solely on the outcome.

Safety and well-being should always be a priority in VR. Take breaks regularly to avoid fatigue and prevent motion sickness. Stay hydrated and ensure your physical environment is safe and clear of obstacles. Be aware of your surroundings in both the real and virtual worlds. Responsible VR usage contributes to a more enjoyable and sustainable experience. Listen to your body and take breaks when needed.

Community involvement can enrich your multiplayer VR journey. Join online forums, connect with other VR enthusiasts, and participate in events. Sharing your experiences, tips, and insights can create a sense of belonging and foster valuable connections. Engaging with the wider VR community can lead to new friendships, collaborative opportunities, and a deeper understanding of the evolving landscape of virtual reality. The sense of community adds another layer to the immersive experience.

Expanding your VR horizons through continuous exploration and experimentation is essential. The field of virtual reality is constantly evolving, with new experiences and technologies emerging regularly. Stay curious, embrace the unknown, and be open to trying new things. This ongoing exploration will keep your VR experiences fresh and exciting. Keeping up with the latest developments in VR technology can enhance your enjoyment and open up new possibilities. By actively participating in the evolving world of VR, you contribute to its growth and development. Embrace the journey and the ever-expanding possibilities it offers.

2.2 The Challenge of Real-Time

The relentless ticking of the clock presents a unique set of constraints and opportunities. Real-time systems demand immediate reactions, split-second decisions, and a constant awareness of the present moment. This immediacy, while challenging, unlocks a world of possibilities, from interactive entertainment to life-saving medical devices. Understanding the nuances of real-time operations is crucial for navigating this dynamic landscape.

One of the core tenets of real-time systems is responsiveness. A delayed reaction can have significant consequences, ranging from a frustrating user experience in a video game to critical failures in industrial control systems.

Think of a self-driving car: its ability to react instantly to pedestrians, other vehicles, and changing road conditions is paramount for safety. This responsiveness is measured in latency, the time elapsed between an input event and the system's corresponding output. Minimizing latency is a constant battle fought on multiple fronts, including hardware optimization, efficient algorithms, and streamlined communication protocols.

Data acquisition plays a vital role in the real-time equation. Systems must gather information from the environment, process it, and act upon it, all within stringent time constraints. Consider a high-frequency trading platform. It ingests a constant stream of market data, analyzes it for profitable opportunities, and executes trades in milliseconds. The accuracy and speed of data acquisition directly impact the system's performance and effectiveness. This often necessitates specialized hardware, like high-speed sensors and dedicated data acquisition cards, coupled with optimized software routines for efficient data handling.

Predictability becomes paramount in the realm of real-time systems. Jitter, the unpredictable variation in latency, can introduce instability and compromise performance. Imagine a robotic surgical arm experiencing inconsistent delays in its movements. The consequences could be disastrous. Therefore, real-time systems strive for deterministic behavior, ensuring that operations complete within predictable timeframes. This requires careful management of system resources, prioritization of critical tasks, and meticulous testing to identify and mitigate sources of jitter.

Resource management is another critical aspect. Real-time systems often operate under tight resource constraints, whether it's limited processing power, memory capacity, or communication bandwidth. Efficiently allocating and utilizing these resources is essential for maintaining responsiveness and predictability. Techniques like pre-allocation of memory, task scheduling algorithms, and optimized data structures can significantly enhance system performance. Consider a real-time operating system (RTOS) managing a complex network of sensors and actuators. The RTOS must dynamically allocate resources, prioritize critical tasks, and ensure that all deadlines are met.

Synchronization and communication between different components of a real-time system introduce additional complexities. Data must flow seamlessly between sensors, processors, and actuators, all while adhering to strict timing requirements. Imagine a distributed control system managing a power grid. Precise synchronization between different control units is essential for maintaining grid stability and preventing blackouts. Robust communication protocols, time synchronization mechanisms, and careful system design are necessary to ensure efficient and reliable data exchange.

Fault tolerance and resilience are also paramount considerations. Real-time systems often operate in critical environments where failures can have severe consequences. Mechanisms for detecting and recovering from errors are crucial for maintaining system stability and preventing catastrophic failures. Redundancy in hardware and software, error detection codes, and fail-safe mechanisms can enhance the system's robustness and ensure continuous operation even in the face of unforeseen events. Consider a flight control system: redundant sensors, backup processors, and failover mechanisms are essential for ensuring the safety of the aircraft.

Testing and validation of real-time systems present unique challenges. Traditional testing methods may not be adequate for capturing the dynamic behavior and timing constraints of these systems. Specialized testing tools and techniques, such as real-time simulators, hardware-in-the-loop testing, and performance analysis tools, are necessary for thoroughly evaluating system behavior and ensuring that it meets the stringent requirements of real-time operation. Think about testing the software for a pacemaker. Rigorous testing under simulated real-world conditions is essential for verifying its reliability and safety.

The development of real-time systems demands a meticulous approach, careful consideration of timing constraints, and a deep understanding of the underlying hardware and software. From the initial design stages to the final testing and deployment, every aspect of the development process must be geared towards achieving responsiveness, predictability, and robustness. This often necessitates specialized skills and expertise in areas such as real-time operating systems, embedded systems, and communication protocols. The challenges are significant, but the potential rewards are immense, unlocking a world of possibilities in diverse fields, from medical devices and industrial automation to gaming and entertainment.

Finally, the evolving landscape of technology continues to present new opportunities and challenges for real-time systems. The emergence of new hardware platforms, communication technologies, and software tools is constantly pushing the boundaries of what is possible. Staying abreast of these advancements is crucial for developing cutting-edge real-time systems that meet the ever-increasing demands of our increasingly interconnected world. This ongoing evolution requires continuous learning, adaptation, and a commitment to innovation.

2.3 Asynchronous Solutions

Imagine a bustling kitchen. Multiple chefs work simultaneously, each focused on their own task – chopping vegetables, stirring sauces, grilling meat. They don't need to wait for one another to finish before starting their part of the meal preparation. This, in essence, is asynchronous programming: independent processes working concurrently without blocking each other. It's a powerful tool for creating responsive and efficient applications, particularly crucial in handling tasks like network requests or file I/O.

Consider a scenario where your application needs to fetch data from a remote server. With a synchronous approach, your application would halt all other operations while waiting for the server to respond. This leads to a frustrating user experience, with frozen screens and unresponsive interfaces. Asynchronous programming offers a solution. By delegating the network request to a separate process, your application can continue executing other tasks, remaining responsive to user input while the data is fetched in the background. Once the data arrives, the application is notified and can process it.

This concept of delegating tasks and receiving notifications is fundamental to understanding asynchronous solutions. We often use mechanisms like callbacks, promises, and async/await to manage this flow. A callback is a function that's executed once a specific task is complete. Think of it as leaving a note for someone to call you back once they've finished a job. Promises represent the eventual result of an asynchronous operation, allowing you to handle success or failure scenarios more elegantly. Async/await builds upon promises, providing a more synchronous-looking syntax for asynchronous code, making it easier to read and reason about.

Let's delve into a practical example. Imagine building a weather application. You need to fetch weather data from an API for multiple cities. Using an asynchronous approach, you can initiate requests for each city concurrently. As each request completes, a callback function is triggered, updating the corresponding section of your user interface with the retrieved data. This approach significantly reduces the overall time it takes to display all the weather information, providing a much smoother and more responsive experience for the user.

Implementing asynchronous solutions effectively often involves careful consideration of concurrency control mechanisms. Imagine multiple processes trying to update the same piece of data simultaneously. This can lead to data corruption and unexpected behavior. To prevent this, we employ techniques like locks, mutexes, and semaphores. These mechanisms ensure that only one process can access a shared resource at a time, maintaining data integrity. Choosing the right concurrency control mechanism depends on the specific requirements of your application and the level of granularity needed.

Another key aspect of asynchronous programming is error handling. Because asynchronous operations run independently, errors might occur in the background without immediately disrupting the main application flow. Therefore, robust error handling is crucial. This often involves using try-catch blocks within asynchronous functions and handling potential exceptions gracefully. Proper error handling not only prevents application crashes but also provides valuable information for debugging and improving the reliability of your code.

When designing asynchronous solutions, it's important to consider the trade-offs involved. While asynchronous programming can greatly improve responsiveness and efficiency, it can also introduce complexity. Managing multiple concurrent processes and handling their interactions can be challenging. Debugging asynchronous code can also be more difficult, as the execution flow is not always linear. However, the benefits of improved performance and responsiveness often outweigh these challenges, especially in modern applications that deal with a large volume of data and user interactions.

A deeper understanding of the underlying mechanisms of asynchronous operations can greatly benefit developers. Consider the event loop, a core component of many asynchronous frameworks. The event loop continuously monitors for completed asynchronous operations and executes their associated callbacks or resolves their promises. This allows the main application thread to remain free to handle other tasks, ensuring responsiveness. Familiarizing yourself with the specifics of the event loop in your chosen framework can help you write more efficient and predictable asynchronous code.

Asynchronous programming offers various patterns for structuring your code. One common pattern is the producer-consumer model, where one process (the producer) generates data, and another process (the consumer) processes it. This pattern is often used in scenarios like handling streams of data or processing messages from a queue. Another pattern is the task-based approach, where you define individual tasks that are executed asynchronously. This allows for greater flexibility and control over the execution flow.

Finally, remember that choosing the right asynchronous approach depends on the specific context of your project. Consider the nature of the tasks you need to perform, the performance requirements, and the complexity of the interactions between different parts of your application. By carefully evaluating these factors, you can choose the asynchronous solution that best suits your needs, leading to a more responsive, efficient, and robust application. Don't be afraid to experiment with different approaches and find what works best for your specific use case. The world of asynchronous programming is vast and constantly evolving, offering exciting possibilities for building modern, high-performance applications.

3 Crafting Immersive Narratives

Presence, agency, and transformation: these are the cornerstones of effective VR storytelling. Think of traditional storytelling as presenting a finished tapestry. In VR, you're offering the user a loom and threads, empowering them to weave their own experience within the parameters you define. This interactivity elevates engagement beyond passive observation, fostering a sense of ownership over the narrative. Consider the difference between watching a film about climbing Mount Everest and virtually scaling the mountain yourself. The latter, while simulated, offers a visceral connection, a sense of accomplishment that resonates on a deeper level. This active participation, however, demands a different approach to narrative design. It's less about dictating a linear path and more about crafting a world rich with possibilities, allowing the user's choices to shape the unfolding story.

One potent technique for achieving this is environmental storytelling. Instead of relying solely on exposition, weave the narrative into the fabric of the virtual world. Let the environment itself reveal the story. A dilapidated building, scarred with the remnants of a past conflict, can speak volumes about the history of a place without a single line of dialogue. A child's drawing tucked away in a drawer, a half-written letter on a desk, or the faint melody of a distant song can provide glimpses into the lives of characters and enrich the narrative tapestry. These subtle details invite exploration and reward curiosity, drawing the user deeper into the experience. They allow for individual interpretation, creating a personalized narrative journey for each user.

User agency is paramount. Empowering the user to make meaningful choices, however small, enhances their sense of presence and deepens their investment in the narrative. These choices needn't always be grand, life-or-death decisions. Even simple interactions, like choosing which path to take through a forest or deciding whether to open a mysterious box, can contribute to a feeling of agency. The key is ensuring that these choices have consequences, however subtle, that ripple through the experience. Perhaps choosing one path leads to a hidden encounter, while another reveals a crucial piece of information. This interconnectedness of choices and outcomes creates a dynamic and personalized narrative experience.

Emotional engagement in VR transcends the intellectual connection we experience with traditional storytelling mediums. By leveraging the immersive nature of VR, you can tap into the user's emotions on a visceral level. Imagine a scenario where the user must comfort a grieving virtual character. The act of reaching out, offering a virtual hand of support, can evoke a powerful emotional response in the user, fostering empathy and connection. This heightened emotional engagement is a unique strength of VR storytelling. Carefully consider how sensory stimuli – sound, visuals, even haptic feedback – can be orchestrated to create specific emotional responses. The rustle of leaves, the warmth of a virtual campfire, the subtle vibration of a controller – these sensory details can profoundly impact the user's emotional experience.

Looking towards the future of VR storytelling, consider the potential of artificial characters driven by advanced AI. Imagine interacting with virtual characters who respond realistically to your actions and choices, adapting their behavior and dialogue dynamically. This level of interactivity could blur the lines between reality and simulation, creating truly immersive and unpredictable narrative experiences. Further, the integration of biometric feedback could personalize narratives in unprecedented ways. Imagine a story that adapts to your heart rate, your breathing, even your emotional state. Such advancements could usher in a new era of personalized storytelling, where the narrative responds to and reflects the user's unique inner world.

Consider the implications of procedural generation for creating vast and dynamic virtual worlds. Imagine exploring a landscape that evolves in response to your actions, where every choice you make shapes the environment around you. This dynamic interplay between user and environment could create a sense of wonder and discovery, fostering a truly personalized and ever-changing narrative experience. The possibilities are boundless, and the future of VR storytelling is ripe with potential. As you embark on your own VR narrative journeys, remember to prioritize presence, agency, and transformation. Empower your users to become active participants in the story, to shape their own experiences, and to emerge from the virtual world transformed. By embracing these principles, you can unlock the true potential of VR storytelling and create experiences that resonate deeply with your audience.

3.1 Storytelling in Virtual Reality

Immersion, that's the magic word in virtual reality. And what better way to achieve truly deep immersion than through compelling storytelling? VR offers a unique opportunity to place the user inside the narrative, making them an active participant rather than a passive observer. This shift necessitates a different approach to storytelling, one that considers the user's agency and the 360-degree environment. Think of it as crafting an experience, not just a linear tale.

One crucial aspect of VR storytelling is presence. You want the user to truly believe they are there, within the story world. This involves meticulous attention to detail in the environment. From the rustling of leaves in a virtual forest to the echo in a grand cathedral, sound design plays a pivotal role. Similarly, visual elements must be carefully considered. Realistic lighting, textures, and object interactions all contribute to a believable and engaging experience. Remember, the user can look anywhere, so every element of the scene should contribute to the story. A forgotten prop in a dark corner or a poorly textured surface can shatter the illusion just as easily as a jarring plot hole.

Consider the unique affordances of the medium. VR allows for interaction in ways traditional storytelling can't. Let users manipulate objects, solve puzzles, and make choices that influence the narrative. This interactivity fosters a sense of agency, making the story more personal and memorable. However, be cautious about overwhelming the user with too many choices. Carefully guide their interactions, offering meaningful choices that impact the story's trajectory without creating decision paralysis. A well-placed interactive element can be far more effective than a barrage of options.

Point of view (POV) is another key consideration. Will your story be told from a first-person or third-person perspective? Each has its own strengths and weaknesses. First-person offers the most immersive experience, placing the user directly into the protagonist's shoes. This allows for a deep connection with the character and story world. However, it can also limit the narrative scope. Third-person, on the other hand, allows for a broader perspective and more cinematic storytelling techniques. You can control the camera, showing the user things the protagonist might not see. The choice ultimately depends on the specific story you're trying to tell.

Character development in VR requires a nuanced approach. Since users are often embodied within the story, traditional character exposition can feel clunky and unnatural. Show, don't tell. Reveal character through actions, interactions, and subtle environmental cues. A nervously tapping foot, a hesitant glance, a cluttered workspace \item these small details can speak volumes. Allow users to infer character traits through observation and interaction, creating a more organic and believable experience.

Think beyond linear narratives. VR offers the opportunity to explore non-linear storytelling, where users can discover the story at their own pace and in their own order. This can create a sense of exploration and discovery, encouraging repeat playthroughs. Imagine a virtual museum where each exhibit tells a piece of a larger story, or a mysterious island where users can uncover hidden clues and unravel a centuries-old mystery. The possibilities are endless.

Embrace the power of spatial audio. Sound in VR isn't just about creating a realistic soundscape; it can also be used to guide the user's attention and enhance the narrative. A whisper from behind can create a sense of unease, while a distant melody can draw the user towards a specific location. Use spatial audio to create a dynamic and immersive soundscape that complements the visuals and enhances the story.

Don't forget the emotional impact. VR has the power to evoke strong emotions in users, leveraging the immersive environment to create truly memorable experiences. Whether you're aiming for joy, fear, or sadness, consider how the various elements of your VR experience – visuals, sound, interaction, and narrative – work together to create the desired emotional response. A well-crafted VR story can transport users to another world and leave a lasting impression.

Test and iterate. As with any form of storytelling, the key to success in VR is to test your experience thoroughly and iterate based on user feedback. Observe how users interact with your story, identify any pain points, and make adjustments as needed. This iterative process is crucial for refining the experience and ensuring it delivers the intended impact.

Finally, consider the ethical implications of your story. VR is a powerful medium, and it's important to use it responsibly. Be mindful of the potential for discomfort or distress, particularly when dealing with sensitive subject matter. Provide clear warnings and allow users to easily exit the experience if they feel overwhelmed. By considering these ethical considerations, you can create a safe and enjoyable experience for all users. Embrace the power of VR storytelling, and you'll unlock a new dimension of narrative immersion.

3.2 Interactive Narratives

Choosing the right path for your interactive narrative can feel like navigating a labyrinth. Each decision point, each branching storyline, represents a potential fork in the road, and the success of your project hinges on carefully guiding your audience through this intricate network. The most effective interactive narratives don't just offer choices; they craft an experience where every decision feels meaningful and impactful. This sense of agency is crucial. It transforms passive readers into active participants, invested in the unfolding story and eager to discover the consequences of their actions.

Consider the structure of your narrative. Will you employ a linear structure with occasional choices, or will you embrace a more complex, web-like design where each decision opens up a multitude of possibilities? A linear approach can be beneficial for beginners, offering a manageable scope while still allowing for player agency. More complex structures, however, offer the potential for richer, more replayable experiences, although they demand careful planning and execution to avoid becoming overwhelming or incoherent.

Another crucial element is the pacing of your narrative. Just as in traditional storytelling, the rhythm and flow of information are key to maintaining audience engagement. In interactive narratives, this involves carefully balancing moments of choice with periods of exposition and character development. Too many choices in rapid succession can lead to decision fatigue, while long stretches without meaningful interaction can cause players to lose interest. Finding the sweet spot is crucial. Think about how you can use pacing to create tension, suspense, and a sense of momentum.

Crafting compelling characters is equally important in interactive narratives. Give your audience characters they can connect with, characters whose motivations and desires they understand, even if they don't necessarily agree with them. This connection will deepen their investment in the story and make their choices feel more significant. Remember, in an interactive narrative, the audience isn't just observing the characters; they're influencing their fates. This connection fosters a sense of shared responsibility and makes the outcomes of the story, both positive and negative, more impactful.

Think about the different perspectives you could offer. Allowing players to experience the story through the eyes of different characters can add layers of complexity and understanding. This technique can also increase replayability, encouraging the audience to explore different perspectives and unravel the narrative from multiple angles. By understanding the motivations and biases of different characters, players can gain a deeper appreciation for the nuances of the story and the consequences of their choices.

The medium you choose to deliver your interactive narrative also plays a significant role. Will it be a text-based adventure, a visual novel, or a fully realized 3D game? Each medium has its own strengths and limitations. Consider your target audience and the resources available to you. A simple text-based game can be highly effective if it has a compelling story and well-written prose. Visual novels can add an extra layer of immersion with artwork and music. More complex mediums, like 3D games, offer greater potential for interactivity but require significantly more development time and resources. Choose the medium that best suits your story and your capabilities.

Don't underestimate the power of feedback. Testing your interactive narrative with a diverse group of players can provide invaluable insights. Observe how they interact with your story, which choices they make, and how they react to the consequences. This feedback can help you identify areas where the narrative might be unclear, confusing, or unbalanced. Use this information to refine your story, improve the pacing, and ensure that the choices feel meaningful and impactful. Iterative development, incorporating feedback and refining your work, is crucial for creating a truly engaging and satisfying interactive narrative.

Consider incorporating elements of mystery and intrigue. Unraveling a complex plot or uncovering hidden secrets can be a powerful motivator for players. Drop hints and clues throughout the narrative, encouraging players to explore and investigate. The sense of discovery and the satisfaction of piecing together the puzzle can add a significant layer of enjoyment to the experience. Think about how you can use foreshadowing and red herrings to keep players guessing and engaged.

Remember, choice architecture is crucial. The way you present choices to your audience can significantly influence their decisions. Consider the wording, the context, and the potential consequences of each option. Avoid overwhelming players with too many choices at once. Instead, focus on presenting meaningful decisions that have a clear impact on the story. The goal is to create a sense of agency, where players feel like their choices truly matter.

Finally, consider the overall theme and message you want to convey. What do you want your audience to take away from the experience? Interactive narratives, like any form of storytelling, can be a powerful tool for exploring complex themes and prompting reflection. Use your narrative to explore ideas, challenge assumptions, and spark conversations. By weaving a compelling story and offering meaningful choices, you can create an experience that resonates with your audience long after they've finished playing.

3.3 The Role of the User

Understanding the user is paramount. Their needs, motivations, and behaviors shape every aspect of a successful product. Without a deep understanding of the user, we're building in the dark, hoping for a lucky hit rather than strategically targeting a real need. Consider this chapter your compass, guiding you toward user-centric design and development. It's about putting the user firmly at the helm, steering your project towards success.

Think about the last time you used a product that truly delighted you. What made it stand out? Chances are, it seamlessly addressed a specific need, effortlessly guided you through its functionalities, and left you feeling satisfied and accomplished. This positive experience wasn't an accident. It was the direct result of a design process that prioritized the user. Every button, every interaction, every piece of feedback was carefully crafted with the user in mind. This chapter delves into the essential strategies for achieving this user-focused approach. We'll explore how to identify your target audience, understand their motivations, and translate those insights into a product that resonates.

Defining your target user isn't simply about demographics. While age, location, and occupation provide a basic framework, they only scratch the surface. Instead, we need to dive deeper into the user's psychographics – their values, interests, and aspirations. What motivates them? What are their pain points? What solutions are they currently using, and what frustrations do they experience? By answering these questions, you begin to paint a rich, nuanced picture of your ideal user. This allows you to move beyond broad generalizations and focus on the specific needs and desires that drive their behavior.

Once you've identified your target user, the next step is to gather insights. This involves employing a variety of research methods, each offering unique perspectives. User interviews, for example, provide rich qualitative data, allowing you to explore the "why" behind user behaviors. Surveys can reach a wider audience, providing quantitative data to validate your assumptions. Observational studies offer a glimpse into real-world usage, revealing how users interact with your product in their natural environment. A/B testing allows you to compare different design choices and measure their impact on user behavior. By combining these methods, you can build a comprehensive understanding of your user's needs and preferences.

Translating user insights into actionable design decisions requires careful consideration. It's not simply about incorporating every feature request or addressing every complaint. It's about prioritizing the most impactful changes and aligning them with your overall product vision. Consider the user journey map, a visualization of the steps a user takes to achieve a specific goal. By mapping out this journey, you can identify potential pain points and opportunities for improvement. Think about each touchpoint, each interaction, and ask yourself: How can we make this experience more seamless, more intuitive, and more enjoyable for the user?

Empathy plays a crucial role in this process. Stepping into your user's shoes allows you to see the world from their perspective. It helps you understand their frustrations, their motivations, and their unmet needs. By cultivating empathy, you can design solutions that genuinely address their challenges and enhance their experience. Remember, the user is not a statistic or a data point; they are a real person with real needs and desires. Treat them as such.

Iterative design is essential for creating user-centered products. It's a cyclical process of designing, testing, and refining. By constantly seeking feedback and iterating on your designs, you can ensure that your product remains aligned with user needs. Don't be afraid to experiment, to try new approaches, and to learn from your mistakes. The goal is to continuously improve the user experience, making your product more valuable and more enjoyable with each iteration.

Building a user-centered product is not a one-time event; it's an ongoing commitment. The user landscape is constantly evolving, with new technologies, new trends, and new expectations emerging all the time. Staying ahead of these changes requires constant vigilance and a willingness to adapt. Regularly revisit your user research, gather feedback, and iterate on your designs. By embracing this continuous improvement mindset, you can ensure that your product remains relevant, engaging, and valuable to your users.

Remember, the user is not just a consumer of your product; they are a partner in its development. By actively involving them in the design process, you can create products that truly meet their needs and exceed their expectations. This collaborative approach not only results in better products but also fosters a sense of ownership and loyalty among your users.

Consider the long-term impact of user-centric design. A product that truly resonates with users will not only generate revenue but also build brand loyalty and advocacy. Satisfied users become your biggest champions, spreading the word and attracting new customers. By prioritizing the user, you are investing in the long-term success of your product and your business. This investment will pay dividends in the form of increased engagement, higher retention rates, and a stronger brand reputation.

3.4 Emotional Engagement in VR

Presence, that uncanny feeling of "being there" inside a virtual environment, is often cited as the holy grail of VR development. But true immersion isn't just about convincing our senses; it's about captivating our emotions. It's about forging a connection that transcends the digital and resonates with our human experience. Building this emotional engagement is crucial for creating memorable and impactful VR experiences.

One powerful technique for fostering emotional connection is through narrative. Storytelling is deeply ingrained in human nature. We are wired to respond to narratives, to empathize with characters, and to become invested in their journeys. In VR, we have the opportunity to place the user directly inside the story, transforming them from passive observer to active participant. This shift in perspective can dramatically amplify the emotional impact of the narrative. Consider the difference between watching a film about a refugee crisis and experiencing it firsthand in VR, walking through a refugee camp, interacting with displaced families, and hearing their stories. The immersive nature of VR allows us to connect with the human element of the story on a much deeper level.

Character development is essential to driving emotional engagement in VR narratives. Compelling characters with relatable motivations, flaws, and strengths can draw users into the experience and foster a sense of connection. Think about how you can use body language, facial expressions, and voice acting to create believable and emotionally resonant characters. Subtle details can make a significant difference. A slight tremor in a character's voice during a moment of vulnerability can be more powerful than any dramatic monologue. Give your characters agency within the narrative, allowing the user to influence their actions and relationships. This sense of shared experience can further solidify the emotional bond between the user and the virtual world.

Environmental storytelling can also play a significant role in shaping emotional responses. The environment is not just a backdrop; it's an integral part of the narrative. Every detail, from the lighting and sound design to the placement of objects and the overall atmosphere, can contribute to the emotional tone of the experience. Imagine exploring a dilapidated, overgrown mansion in VR. The creaking floorboards, flickering lights, and dusty portraits on the wall can create a sense of unease and mystery, even before any explicit narrative events unfold. Consider how you can use environmental cues to foreshadow events, reveal character backstories, and evoke specific emotions in the user.

Sound design is often an overlooked but crucial element of emotional engagement in VR. Sound has a profound impact on our emotions and can be used to create a sense of immersion, heighten tension, and evoke specific feelings. The rustling of leaves in a virtual forest, the distant rumble of thunder, the gentle lapping of waves on a virtual shore – these subtle soundscapes can create a powerful sense of presence and enhance the emotional impact of the experience. Spatial audio, which allows sounds to be positioned in 3D space, can further enhance the realism and immersiveness of the VR environment. Imagine hearing a whisper directly behind you in VR, turning around, and finding no one there. The combination of spatial audio and visual cues can create a truly chilling and memorable experience.

Music is another powerful tool for evoking emotion. A soaring orchestral score can amplify a moment of triumph, while a melancholic melody can underscore a scene of loss. However, it's important to use music judiciously. Too much music can be overwhelming and detract from the experience. Silence can also be incredibly effective in VR, allowing natural sounds and dialogue to take center stage and create a more intimate and emotionally resonant experience.

Haptic feedback, the use of tactile sensations to enhance the VR experience, can also contribute to emotional engagement. Imagine reaching out to touch a virtual object and feeling the texture and weight of it in your hand. This sense of physical interaction can increase the sense of presence and make the virtual world feel more real. Haptic feedback can also be used to create emotional responses. A gentle vibration can simulate a heartbeat, while a sharp jolt can simulate a sudden impact.

Interactivity is at the heart of VR. Unlike traditional media, VR allows users to actively participate in the experience, making choices and influencing the narrative. This sense of agency can significantly enhance emotional engagement. When users feel like they have control over their actions and their impact on the virtual world, they become more invested in the experience and more emotionally connected to the outcome. Give users meaningful choices that affect the story and the characters. Allow them to explore the virtual environment at their own pace and discover hidden details. This sense of freedom and exploration can further deepen their emotional connection to the VR experience.

Ultimately, emotional engagement in VR is about creating experiences that resonate with the human spirit. By carefully crafting narratives, developing compelling characters, designing immersive environments, utilizing sound and music effectively, incorporating haptic feedback, and empowering users with interactivity, we can create VR experiences that are not just visually stunning but also emotionally impactful. These experiences have the potential to transport us to new worlds, connect us with others in profound ways, and transform the way we tell stories and experience the world around us.

3.5 Future of VR Storytelling

Immersive narratives are poised to revolutionize how we experience stories. Virtual Reality (VR) offers a unique opportunity to step inside the narrative, becoming an active participant rather than a passive observer. This shift from observing to experiencing has profound implications for the future of storytelling, impacting everything from character development to plot structure. Imagine not just watching a character's emotional journey but feeling it alongside them, embedded within their world. This level of engagement opens up exciting new possibilities for creators to connect with their audiences on a deeper, more visceral level.

The potential of VR storytelling extends beyond simple immersion. Consider the power of agency within these virtual worlds. No longer bound by a predetermined camera angle or narrative path, the audience can explore, interact, and even influence the unfolding story. This interactivity creates a personalized narrative experience, where choices have consequences and each journey through the story is unique. Imagine a mystery where you, the viewer, can choose which clues to follow, leading to different outcomes and revelations. This level of agency transforms the audience from passive recipients to active co-creators of the narrative.

This shift towards interactive storytelling necessitates a reimagining of traditional narrative structures. Linear narratives, with their fixed beginning, middle, and end, may give way to more dynamic, branching narratives. Think of a choose-your-own-adventure book, but elevated to a fully realized, three-dimensional experience. In this new paradigm, storytellers become architects of experience, crafting intricate worlds with multiple pathways and outcomes, empowering the audience to shape their own journey through the narrative.

Character development also undergoes a transformation in the realm of VR. Proximity and interaction foster a sense of connection and empathy that transcends the traditional screen barrier. Imagine standing face-to-face with a character, witnessing their subtle expressions and body language firsthand. This intimate perspective allows for a deeper understanding of their motivations, fears, and aspirations. Furthermore, the ability to interact with characters, making choices that impact their actions and relationships, creates a sense of shared experience and emotional investment. World-building takes on a new dimension in VR. Immersive environments become more than just backdrops; they become integral to the storytelling process. Imagine exploring a bustling marketplace, feeling the energy of the crowd and the textures of the goods on display, or traversing a desolate wasteland, the wind whipping past you as you struggle to survive. These sensory details create a powerful sense of presence and verisimilitude, drawing the audience deeper into the narrative world.

However, realizing the full potential of VR storytelling requires addressing certain challenges. Technical limitations, such as processing power and resolution, can impact the sense of immersion and realism. Furthermore, designing compelling interactive experiences that seamlessly blend agency with narrative coherence requires careful consideration. Balancing player freedom with a compelling narrative arc is a delicate act, requiring innovative approaches to story structure and game design.

Motion sickness and accessibility are also significant concerns. The immersive nature of VR can induce discomfort in some users, limiting their ability to fully engage with the experience. Ensuring accessibility for individuals with disabilities is crucial for creating truly inclusive storytelling experiences. Developing intuitive control schemes and accommodating diverse physical needs are essential steps towards making VR narratives accessible to everyone.

Despite these challenges, the future of VR storytelling is bright. As technology continues to advance, the barriers to entry are lowering, making VR more accessible to both creators and audiences. This democratization of VR technology is fostering a wave of innovation, with independent creators pushing the boundaries of immersive storytelling. From interactive documentaries to immersive theater experiences, VR is opening up new avenues for creative expression and audience engagement.

The convergence of VR with other emerging technologies, such as augmented reality (AR) and artificial intelligence, further expands the possibilities. Imagine a world where virtual characters interact seamlessly with the real world, blurring the lines between fiction and reality. This blended reality experience could revolutionize fields like education, training, and entertainment, creating immersive and engaging experiences that transcend traditional boundaries.

The evolution of VR storytelling is not just about technological advancements; it's about a fundamental shift in how we experience and engage with narratives. It's about moving from passive observation to active participation, from consuming stories to co-creating them. As VR technology matures and becomes more accessible, we can expect to see a proliferation of innovative and immersive narrative experiences that will transform the way we tell and experience stories for generations to come. This new frontier of storytelling holds immense potential, not just for entertainment, but also for education, empathy building, and exploring the very nature of human experience. The journey into the future of VR storytelling has just begun, and the possibilities are truly limitless.

4 The Symphony of Code

A virtual world, however fantastical, adheres to rules. These rules, the laws of physics governing how objects interact, are not dictated by gravity or friction as we know them, but by lines of code within a physics engine. These engines are the unsung heroes of immersive VR experiences, transforming abstract algorithms into tangible, interactive simulations. They bridge the gap between the ethereal world of code and the visceral experience of the user, allowing us to pick up a virtual object and feel its weight, or witness a crumbling wall cascade with realistic debris. Consider the seemingly simple act of dropping a ball in a virtual environment. Without a physics engine, the ball might simply hover or vanish. With a physics engine, the ball accelerates towards the ground, bounces with a satisfying thud, and eventually settles, its movement dictated by calculated forces of gravity, friction, and restitution.

The complexity of these calculations goes far beyond basic Newtonian physics. Modern physics engines account for a multitude of factors including collision detection, rigid body dynamics, soft body dynamics, and even fluid simulations. Collision detection, for example, is crucial for creating believable interactions. It's the algorithm that determines whether two objects are intersecting, triggering subsequent reactions based on their properties. Imagine a sword clashing against a shield in a VR game. The precise point of contact, the force of the impact, and the resulting deflection are all meticulously calculated by the physics engine, transforming a simple button press into a visceral experience. Without this intricate dance of calculations, the interaction would feel hollow and unconvincing.

Furthermore, the choice of a specific physics engine heavily influences the overall feel of a VR experience. Different engines offer varying strengths and weaknesses, from the highly realistic simulations of engines like Havok, known for its robust handling of complex interactions and destructible environments, to the more performant, albeit less detailed, calculations offered by simpler physics engines designed for mobile VR experiences. This balance between realism and performance is a constant negotiation for VR developers. A visually stunning simulation, burdened by excessive calculations, can lead to performance hiccups, breaking the sense of immersion. Conversely, an overly simplified physics model, while performant, can feel unrealistic and detract from the experience.

Networking, the invisible thread connecting users in shared virtual spaces, plays a crucial role in the asynchronous symphony of code. It's the technology that allows us to interact with others in virtual worlds, sharing experiences and collaborating on tasks, even when separated by vast geographical distances. While real-time communication remains the gold standard for many online interactions, the demands of VR introduce unique challenges. Maintaining consistent, low-latency communication between multiple users in a complex virtual environment requires significant bandwidth and computational power. This becomes especially challenging in asynchronous VR experiences where users may enter and exit the virtual space at different times.

Therefore, robust networking solutions are vital for maintaining consistency and preventing discrepancies between user experiences. Imagine a collaborative VR workspace where multiple users are manipulating shared virtual objects. A robust networking system ensures that each user sees the same object in the same position, even if they interact with it at different times. This synchronization is essential for collaborative tasks, preventing conflicts and ensuring that changes made by one user are reflected accurately for all others. Data persistence is another key aspect of asynchronous networking in VR. The ability to save the state of the virtual world, including object positions, user interactions, and other relevant data, allows users to seamlessly continue their experience later, picking up exactly where they left off.

Finally, the overarching conductor orchestrating this intricate symphony of code is the game engine. Acting as the central nervous system of a VR experience, the game engine brings together all the disparate elements – the physics engine, the networking solutions, the 3D models, the audio, and the user interface – into a cohesive whole. It provides the framework for managing the scene, handling user input, rendering the visuals, and executing the game logic. Choosing the right game engine is a crucial decision for any VR project, influencing not only the development process but also the final user experience. Engines like Unity and Unreal Engine, industry standards in game development, offer robust toolsets and extensive community support, making them popular choices for VR development. Their flexibility allows developers to create a wide range of experiences, from simple interactive simulations to complex, narrative-driven games. The selection of a game engine often depends on the specific requirements of the project. Factors like target platform, performance requirements, visual fidelity, and team expertise all play a role in the decision-making process. For instance, a mobile VR experience might prioritize a lightweight engine optimized for performance on limited hardware, while a high-fidelity simulation might opt for a more powerful engine capable of rendering complex visuals and physics simulations. Ultimately, the game engine serves as the foundation upon which the entire VR experience is built, orchestrating the symphony of code that brings virtual worlds to life. The interplay between these components creates the immersive experiences we associate with virtual reality, transforming lines of code into tangible, interactive realities.

4.1 Game Engines and VR

Stepping into the world of Virtual Reality (VR) development can feel like entering a new dimension. A key to navigating this exciting landscape lies in understanding the powerful tools at your disposal: game engines. These software packages provide the framework, the building blocks, and the interactive elements that bring your VR experiences to life. Choosing the right engine for your project depends on several factors, from your programming proficiency to the specific hardware you're targeting. This exploration of game engines and their application in VR development will equip you with the knowledge to make informed decisions, setting you on the path to crafting compelling virtual worlds.

Two dominant players in the VR game engine arena are Unity and Unreal Engine. Both offer robust features, extensive communities, and a wealth of resources for developers. Unity, known for its user-friendly interface and cross-platform compatibility, provides a smoother entry point for beginners. Its visual scripting system, Bolt, allows creators to build logic without deep coding knowledge, making it accessible to a wider range of users. However, for those seeking maximum visual fidelity and complex simulations, Unreal Engine's power and flexibility are unparalleled. Its Blueprint visual scripting system offers more advanced features than Bolt, allowing for greater customization. The choice between these two powerhouses often comes down to personal preference and project requirements. Investigate the strengths of each engine to determine which best aligns with your vision.

Beyond these two giants, other game engines cater to specific needs within the VR development landscape. Godot, an open-source engine, offers a lightweight and flexible alternative, particularly attractive to independent developers and those seeking greater control over their projects. Its node-based visual scripting system provides a unique approach to game logic creation. CryEngine, renowned for its stunning graphics capabilities, is a strong contender for VR experiences demanding high visual fidelity, though its steeper learning curve may pose a challenge for newcomers. Consider exploring these alternative engines if your project demands a specific feature set or aligns with their strengths.

Once you've selected a game engine, understanding its core components for VR development is crucial. The scene editor acts as your virtual canvas, allowing you to place objects, characters, and environmental elements within your VR world. Manipulating these assets within the 3D space is fundamental to constructing the visual experience. Familiarizing yourself with the engine's physics system allows you to create realistic interactions, such as gravity, collisions, and object manipulation, adding a layer of immersion to the virtual environment. Mastering these core elements is essential for building believable and engaging VR experiences.

Lighting and sound design are critical elements in shaping the atmosphere and immersion of your VR world. Experimenting with different lighting techniques, from ambient lighting to directional light sources, can dramatically impact the mood and visual appeal of your virtual environments. Integrating spatial audio enhances the sense of presence, allowing sounds to emanate from specific locations within the VR space, adding depth and realism to the user experience. Don't underestimate the power of these sensory elements in creating truly captivating VR experiences.

Effective user interface (UI) and user experience (UX) design are paramount in VR development. Traditional UI principles often require adaptation for the immersive nature of VR. Consider the user's field of view and the limitations of interacting with virtual elements. Implementing intuitive navigation systems, clear visual cues, and comfortable interaction methods are essential for a seamless and enjoyable user experience. Prioritize user comfort and accessibility when designing your VR interfaces.

Optimization is crucial for maintaining smooth performance in VR. High frame rates are essential to minimize motion sickness and maintain a sense of immersion. Carefully manage polygon counts, texture sizes, and the complexity of your scenes to ensure optimal performance. Profiling tools within the game engine can identify performance bottlenecks, allowing you to target specific areas for optimization. Regularly test your VR experience on the target hardware to ensure a fluid and responsive experience.

Interactivity is at the heart of compelling VR experiences. Implementing hand tracking allows users to interact with virtual objects directly, enhancing the sense of presence and immersion. Explore the engine's input system to map actions to specific buttons or gestures. Haptic feedback adds another layer of realism, providing tactile sensations that correspond to in-game events. Mastering these interactive elements is key to creating engaging and memorable VR experiences.

Integrating external devices and APIs can extend the capabilities of your VR experiences. Motion capture systems allow for precise tracking of body movements, enabling realistic character animation and immersive interactions. Eye-tracking technology opens new possibilities for user input and interaction, as well as gathering valuable data on user attention and engagement. Explore the integration options provided by your chosen game engine to enhance the functionality and immersion of your VR projects.

Testing and iteration are crucial stages in the VR development process. Regularly test your experience on the target hardware and gather feedback from users. Identify areas for improvement and iterate on your designs based on this feedback. User testing can reveal unforeseen issues and provide valuable insights into the user experience. Embrace this iterative process to refine your VR creation and ensure a polished final product. By mastering these elements and dedicating yourself to continuous improvement, you can unlock the full potential of game engines and bring your VR visions to life.

4.2 Physics Engines: Simulating Reality

The world around us operates on a set of predictable rules: gravity pulls objects downwards, collisions transfer momentum, and objects in motion tend to stay in motion. These physical laws govern everything from the smallest particle to the largest star, and understanding them is key to creating believable simulations in a virtual environment. This is where physics engines come in. They provide a computational framework for mimicking these real-world behaviors, allowing developers to breathe life into digital worlds. Think of a physics engine as a virtual laboratory, a space where the fundamental laws of physics can be applied and manipulated to create interactive experiences.

A physics engine's core function revolves around solving equations. These aren't your typical high-school algebra problems, however. They're complex algorithms that model forces, motion, and collisions. For instance, when a virtual ball bounces, the engine calculates the force of impact, the resulting change in velocity, and the angle of reflection, all in real-time. It then uses these calculations to update the ball's position and trajectory, creating a realistic bouncing motion. Beyond simple bouncing balls, physics engines handle much more sophisticated interactions, from the swaying of cloth to the crumbling of buildings. They can simulate the behavior of rigid bodies, soft bodies, fluids, and even more exotic materials like granular materials like sand.

One crucial concept in physics engine design is collision detection. This is the process of identifying when two or more objects in the simulation come into contact. Without accurate collision detection, objects would simply pass through each other, breaking the illusion of a physical world. There are various techniques for achieving this, ranging from simple bounding box checks to more complex algorithms that analyze the shapes of colliding objects. Consider a racing game, where accurate collision detection is essential for determining the outcome of crashes and ensuring that cars interact realistically with the track and other vehicles.

Another key element is the concept of constraints. Constraints limit the ways in which objects can move and interact. For example, a hinge constraint might be used to connect two objects, allowing them to rotate relative to each other but not separate. This is how you might simulate a door swinging open or a robot arm bending. Different types of constraints, like ball joints, sliders, and springs, offer a wide range of possibilities for creating complex mechanical systems. Imagine building a virtual Rube Goldberg machine: constraints are the glue that holds it all together and dictates how the various parts interact.

Gravity, a fundamental force in our universe, plays a pivotal role in physics simulations. It's the invisible force that pulls objects towards each other, and in a virtual environment, it's responsible for giving objects weight and causing them to fall. The strength of gravity can be adjusted within the simulation, allowing developers to create low-gravity environments like the moon or exaggerate it for comedic effect. Think of a platformer game where the player can adjust the gravity to solve puzzles or reach new areas. Friction, the force that resists motion between surfaces in contact, is another important consideration. It's what allows objects to come to rest and prevents them from sliding endlessly. Physics engines model friction to create realistic interactions between objects and their environment. Imagine a character walking across different surfaces: ice would offer very little friction, causing the character to slip and slide, while concrete would provide much more resistance.

Many game engines integrate physics engines seamlessly into their development environment. This allows developers to easily add physics-based interactions to their games without having to write complex physics code from scratch. This integration opens up a world of creative possibilities, from realistic ragdoll effects to dynamic destruction systems. Imagine a building collapsing realistically in a game, with debris scattering and reacting to the environment, thanks to the underlying physics engine.

Optimizing performance is crucial when dealing with physics simulations. Calculating the interactions of numerous objects in real-time can be computationally intensive. Techniques like spatial partitioning and simplified collision models help to reduce the load on the processor, allowing for larger and more complex simulations. Developers must strike a balance between realism and performance, finding ways to create believable physics without overwhelming the system.

The applications of physics engines extend far beyond gaming. They are used in fields like robotics, engineering, and film animation. In robotics, physics engines help simulate the behavior of robots in different environments, allowing engineers to test and refine their designs before building physical prototypes. In film, they are used to create realistic special effects, from crashing cars to flowing water. The versatility of physics engines makes them a powerful tool for anyone seeking to simulate the physical world.

Beyond the basics, advanced topics in physics engine development include fluid dynamics, soft body simulation, and the implementation of custom constraints. These areas require a deeper understanding of physics and mathematics, but they open up even more possibilities for creating complex and realistic simulations. As you delve deeper into the world of physics engines, you'll discover a vast and ever-evolving field with endless potential for innovation.

4.3 Networking: Connecting Virtual Worlds

The digital landscape is vast and ever-shifting, a complex tapestry woven from connections. For newcomers, navigating this terrain can feel daunting, like stepping into a bustling marketplace with a thousand voices clamoring for attention. It's in these crowded spaces, however, where opportunities lie hidden, waiting to be discovered. Building a strong network within virtual worlds is akin to forging pathways through this marketplace, creating routes to valuable resources, collaborations, and a deeper understanding of the digital realm itself.

These virtual worlds, diverse in their purpose and design, offer a unique environment for networking, unlike anything found in the physical world. They transcend geographical limitations, connecting individuals from across the globe in shared digital spaces. Whether it's a collaborative workspace, a sprawling online game, or a niche forum dedicated to a specific interest, these platforms provide a fertile ground for building connections. The key is to approach these environments strategically, with a clear understanding of how to effectively engage and build meaningful relationships.

Start by identifying the platforms relevant to your goals. What are you hoping to achieve within these virtual worlds? Are you looking for mentorship, collaboration opportunities, or simply to expand your knowledge and understanding of a particular field? Once you've identified your objectives, research the platforms that best align with those goals. Don't spread yourself too thin by trying to be everywhere at once. Focus on a select few platforms where you can invest your time and energy effectively.

Within each chosen platform, actively seek out communities and groups that resonate with your interests. These smaller, more focused groups often provide a more intimate setting for interaction, fostering a sense of belonging and shared purpose. Participate in discussions, offer valuable insights, and ask thoughtful questions. Avoid the temptation to passively consume content; instead, be an active contributor, sharing your own experiences and perspectives. This proactive engagement will make you more visible to others and establish you as a valuable member of the community.

Building a genuine connection goes beyond simply exchanging pleasantries. It requires active listening and a sincere interest in the individuals you interact with. Take the time to learn about their backgrounds, their interests, and their goals. Engage in meaningful conversations that go beyond superficial exchanges. Remember, building a strong network is about fostering mutually beneficial relationships, not just collecting contacts.

The digital environment also offers unique opportunities for showcasing your expertise and building credibility. Share your work, whether it's a blog post, a piece of art, or a coding project, within relevant communities. Offer helpful advice and support to others. By demonstrating your knowledge and skills, you'll naturally attract individuals who are interested in what you have to offer.

Networking in virtual worlds is not a passive endeavor; it requires consistent effort and engagement. Make it a habit to regularly participate in discussions, connect with new individuals, and nurture existing relationships. Just as in the physical world, relationships in the digital realm require ongoing cultivation to flourish.

Remember, networking is a two-way street. Be generous with your time and support, offering assistance to others without expecting anything in return. This spirit of generosity will not only strengthen your existing connections but also attract new opportunities and collaborations.

Don't be afraid to step outside your comfort zone and initiate conversations with individuals you don't know. A simple introduction can often lead to unexpected and valuable connections. Attend virtual events, workshops, and conferences to expand your network and meet new people.

Finally, be mindful of your online presence. Your profile, your contributions to discussions, and your interactions with others all contribute to the overall impression you project. Maintain a professional and respectful demeanor, and be mindful of the language you use. Your online presence is an extension of your professional identity, so ensure it reflects the image you want to convey.

Networking in virtual worlds is a powerful tool for growth and development. By approaching these environments strategically and building genuine connections, you can unlock a wealth of opportunities and navigate the digital landscape with confidence. Embrace the interconnectedness of these virtual spaces, and cultivate relationships that will enrich your journey through the digital realm. Remember, the strength of your network is not just about the number of connections you have, but the quality of those connections and the mutual value you create together. It's about building bridges, fostering collaboration, and creating a supportive community within the vast expanse of the digital world. It's about finding your place within the tapestry and weaving your own unique thread into its intricate design.

5 Designing Virtual Environments

The creation of compelling virtual environments is a multifaceted process, demanding a deep understanding of both artistic principles and technical constraints. Consider the importance of scale and proportion. A towering gothic cathedral evokes awe, while a cramped, cluttered room can induce claustrophobia. Manipulating these elements allows you to control the user's emotional response, guiding them through the narrative or experience you're crafting. This careful manipulation of space extends beyond simple dimensions. The interplay of light and shadow, the use of color theory to evoke specific moods, and the strategic placement of objects all contribute to the overall atmosphere and user experience. Think of each element as a brushstroke in a painting, working together to create a cohesive and immersive world.

Beyond the visual aspects, consider the auditory landscape. Sound design plays a critical role in enhancing immersion. The gentle rustling of leaves in a virtual forest, the distant echo of footsteps in a cavernous hall, or the subtle hum of futuristic machinery all contribute to a richer, more believable environment. Spatial audio, which allows sounds to be positioned in 3D space, is particularly powerful, creating a sense of presence and realism. Imagine hearing a whisper seemingly coming from right behind you in a virtual horror game—a truly immersive experience. Remember, effective sound design is not merely about adding noise; it's about crafting an auditory experience that complements and enhances the visual elements.

User experience (UX) is paramount in virtual environment design. Navigation should be intuitive and seamless, allowing users to explore the virtual world without frustration. Consider incorporating clear visual cues or subtle environmental guidance to direct users towards points of interest. Avoid convoluted pathways or confusing layouts that might disrupt the flow of the experience. Think about how real-world environments guide our movement and apply those principles to your virtual creations. Clear signage, logical pathways, and landmarks all contribute to a smooth and enjoyable user journey.

Optimization is crucial for a smooth and immersive VR experience. High-polygon models and complex textures, while visually appealing, can strain system resources and lead to performance issues like dropped frames and latency. These issues can break immersion and cause discomfort. Employ techniques like level of detail (LOD) switching, which dynamically adjusts the complexity of 3D models based on their distance from the viewer, to maintain a balance between visual fidelity and performance. Occlusion culling, which prevents the rendering of objects hidden from view, is another valuable optimization technique. Consider these techniques as essential tools in your design arsenal, allowing you to create visually rich environments without sacrificing performance.

Creating believable virtual worlds involves more than just visual realism. It's about crafting environments that feel authentic and lived-in. Consider adding details that suggest a history or narrative within the virtual space. A worn rug in a virtual living room, a faded poster on a virtual wall, or a collection of tools in a virtual workshop can all contribute to a sense of realism and depth. These seemingly minor details breathe life into your virtual creations, making them feel more than just empty shells. They tell stories, hint at past events, and add a layer of richness to the overall experience.

Accessibility is a critical consideration in virtual environment design. VR experiences should be inclusive and cater to users with diverse needs and abilities. Consider incorporating features such as adjustable comfort settings, customizable control schemes, and support for assistive technologies. Think about users with physical limitations, visual impairments, or auditory sensitivities. Providing options for locomotion, interaction, and sensory feedback can greatly enhance accessibility and ensure that your virtual creations are enjoyable and usable by a wider audience. Designing for accessibility isn't just about being inclusive; it's about expanding your potential user base and creating a more welcoming and engaging experience for everyone.

The interplay between 3D modeling and level design is fundamental to creating immersive VR environments. A beautifully crafted 3D model of a tree is meaningless without a thoughtfully designed forest to place it in. Level design dictates how users interact with the environment, guiding their exploration and shaping their overall experience. Think of level design as the architectural blueprint of your virtual world, defining the layout, flow, and functionality of the space. A well-designed level should be both aesthetically pleasing and functionally effective, seamlessly integrating the 3D models and other assets to create a cohesive and immersive experience.

The use of real-world architectural principles can greatly enhance the believability of virtual environments. Consider concepts like line of sight, spatial hierarchy, and the use of natural light. These principles can guide the placement of objects, the design of interiors, and the overall layout of the virtual world. Think about how real-world architects use these principles to create functional and aesthetically pleasing spaces. By applying these same principles to your virtual creations, you can imbue them with a sense of realism and familiarity.

The process of creating a virtual environment is an iterative one, involving constant refinement and testing. Don't be afraid to experiment with different approaches, gather feedback from users, and make adjustments along the way. Think of it as sculpting a piece of clay, gradually shaping and refining it until it takes its final form. This iterative process allows you to address any issues with navigation, optimize performance, and ensure that the final product meets your design goals and provides a truly immersive and engaging experience for your users. Embrace the iterative nature of design, and your virtual worlds will flourish.

5.1 3D Modeling for VR

The first step in creating compelling VR experiences often involves building the virtual world itself. This process, known as 3D modeling, is where your creative vision takes shape. It's where you construct the environments, objects, and characters that populate your virtual reality. Choosing the right software is paramount. Several popular programs cater specifically to game development and VR, offering toolsets optimized for real-time performance and interactive elements. Consider factors like ease of use, cost, available tutorials, and community support when making your decision. Exploring different software options and identifying one that aligns with your workflow and skill level is crucial for long-term success. Beginners often feel overwhelmed by the complexity of 3D modeling software. Don't let the initial learning curve discourage you. Start with simple projects, like creating basic geometric shapes. Experiment with the software's interface and familiarize yourself with the navigation controls. Grasping fundamental concepts like manipulating vertices, edges, and faces will lay a solid foundation for more advanced modeling techniques. Numerous online tutorials and resources can guide you through these initial steps, offering step-by-step instructions and practical exercises. Embrace these learning opportunities and practice regularly to build confidence and proficiency.

Once you're comfortable with basic shapes, progress towards creating more complex objects. Consider breaking down complex objects into smaller, simpler components. For example, when modeling a chair, start with the legs, then the seat, and finally the backrest. Combine these individual pieces to create the final model. This modular approach simplifies the process and makes it easier to manage complex geometries. Employ techniques like extrusion, beveling, and subdivision surface modeling to add detail and refine your creations. Remember to maintain a balance between visual fidelity and performance, especially in VR, where optimization is key to a smooth user experience.

Texturing adds depth and realism to your 3D models. Imagine a plain wooden table in your virtual world. Now, picture that same table with visible wood grain, subtle imperfections, and even a few scratches on the surface. That's the power of texturing. Learn how to apply different types of textures, such as diffuse maps for color, normal maps for surface detail, and specular maps for reflectivity. Experiment with various texture mapping techniques, including UV unwrapping, to accurately wrap your textures onto your models. Understanding the principles of texture creation and application can drastically elevate the visual appeal of your VR environments.

Lighting plays a pivotal role in shaping the mood and atmosphere of your virtual world. Just as a well-placed lamp can transform a room in real life, virtual lighting can dramatically impact the user experience in VR. Explore different lighting techniques, such as directional lights, point lights, and ambient lights, to achieve the desired aesthetic. Pay attention to light intensity, color, and shadows to create a sense of depth and realism. Effective lighting can evoke emotions, guide the user's attention, and enhance the overall immersion of the VR experience.

Optimization is essential for achieving smooth performance in VR. High frame rates and low latency are crucial for minimizing motion sickness and maximizing user comfort. Employ techniques like polygon reduction, texture optimization, and level-of-detail modeling to reduce the computational load on the VR system. Consider baking lighting and shadows to further improve performance. Regularly test your VR experience on the target hardware to identify and address any performance bottlenecks. Prioritizing optimization throughout the development process ensures a seamless and enjoyable VR experience for your users.

User interaction is a defining characteristic of VR. Unlike traditional media, VR allows users to actively engage with the virtual environment. Incorporate interactive elements into your 3D models. Consider adding features like buttons, levers, and doors that users can manipulate. Think about how users will interact with objects in your virtual world and design your models accordingly. By enabling meaningful interactions, you transform passive observers into active participants, enhancing their sense of presence and immersion.

Consider the scale and proportions of your 3D models in relation to the user. In VR, the user's virtual body serves as the reference point for experiencing the virtual world. Ensure that objects are appropriately sized and positioned to create a realistic sense of scale. For example, a chair should be the right height for the user to sit on, and a door should be tall enough for the user to walk through. Accurate scaling enhances the user's sense of presence and makes the virtual world feel more believable.

Sound design adds another layer of immersion to your VR experiences. Imagine walking through a virtual forest and hearing the rustling of leaves under your feet, the chirping of birds overhead, and the distant call of an owl. These auditory cues enrich the virtual environment and deepen the user's sense of presence. Explore how to incorporate spatial audio, which simulates the way sound travels in the real world. Experiment with different sound effects and ambient sounds to create a more immersive and engaging VR experience.

Finally, remember that creating compelling VR experiences is an iterative process. Don't be afraid to experiment, make mistakes, and learn from your experiences. Regularly test your VR projects, gather feedback from users, and refine your designs based on their input. Embrace the iterative nature of VR development, and continually strive to improve your skills and create even more immersive and engaging experiences. This ongoing process of refinement is essential for crafting truly captivating VR experiences that resonate with your audience.

5.2 Level Design and User Experience

A well-designed level is more than just a pretty backdrop. It's a carefully crafted experience that guides the player, evokes emotion, and ultimately delivers satisfaction. Think of it as an invisible hand gently nudging the player forward, whispering secrets, and revealing challenges at just the right moment. This delicate balance between challenge and reward, exploration and direction, is the heart of compelling level design. It's the difference between a player feeling accomplished and feeling frustrated.

The first step in crafting a memorable level is understanding your target audience. Who are they? What are their expectations? Are they seasoned gamers hungry for a brutal challenge, or casual players looking for a relaxing escape? Knowing your audience informs every decision you make, from the difficulty curve to the aesthetic style. A horror game aimed at hardcore players might embrace claustrophobic corridors and jump scares, while a puzzle game for a broader audience might opt for bright colors and gentle learning curves. Consider the skills you expect your players to possess and how you can introduce new mechanics gradually without overwhelming them.

Once you understand your audience, you can begin to think about the core loop of your game. This is the sequence of actions the player will repeat throughout the level and, indeed, the entire game. Is it exploration-focused, combat-heavy, or puzzle-based? The core loop dictates the pacing and structure of your levels. A fast-paced action game will demand shorter, more intense levels, while a slower, more narrative-driven game can afford to have longer, more explorative levels. Understanding this core loop helps create a consistent and rewarding player experience.

Now, consider the flow of your level. How do you want the player to move through the space? Do you want them to feel a sense of freedom and exploration, or do you want to guide them along a specific path? Tools like visual cues, environmental storytelling, and strategically placed obstacles can subtly direct the player's attention and encourage them to explore specific areas. A strategically placed light source can draw the player's eye towards a hidden path, while a crumbling wall might suggest a secret passage. These subtle cues create a sense of discovery and reward the player for their curiosity.

Lighting and sound play a crucial role in setting the mood and atmosphere of your level. A dimly lit corridor with flickering lights creates a sense of unease and tension, while a brightly lit open field evokes feelings of peace and tranquility. Sound effects can further enhance the immersion. The distant howl of a wolf in a forest level or the creaking of floorboards in a haunted house can add layers of depth and suspense. Don't underestimate the power of audio to heighten the emotional impact of your level.

Challenge is essential for engagement, but it must be carefully balanced. A level that is too easy will quickly become boring, while one that is too difficult will lead to frustration. Introduce challenges gradually, allowing the player to master new skills and mechanics before throwing them into the deep end. Provide clear feedback and opportunities for the player to learn from their mistakes. A well-placed checkpoint can be a lifeline in a challenging section, allowing the player to retry without losing significant progress. Remember, the goal is to create a sense of accomplishment, not to punish the player.

User experience (UX) is intrinsically linked to level design. Every design choice, from the placement of enemies to the color of the walls, impacts the player's experience. A cluttered and confusing interface can detract from the gameplay, while a clean and intuitive one enhances it. Think about how the player will interact with the game world. Are the controls responsive? Is the camera angle helpful? Is the information presented clearly and concisely? These seemingly small details can make a huge difference in the overall enjoyment of the game.

Testing is crucial. Playtest your levels regularly and gather feedback from a variety of players. Watch how they interact with the environment, where they get stuck, and what they enjoy the most. Don't be afraid to iterate based on this feedback. Sometimes, the smallest changes can have a significant impact on the player experience. Even seasoned designers rely on playtesting to refine their levels and ensure they are fun and engaging.

Consider the narrative implications of your level design. How does the environment contribute to the overall story? A war-torn battlefield tells a different story than a lush, vibrant forest. Use the environment to convey information about the game's world, its history, and its characters. A crumbling statue or a discarded letter can add layers of depth and intrigue to the narrative. Environmental storytelling can enrich the player's experience and make the game world feel more alive.

Finally, remember that level design is an iterative process. It's about constant experimentation, refinement, and a deep understanding of your players. By focusing on creating a compelling and rewarding experience, you can transform a simple level into a truly memorable journey. Embrace the challenge, experiment with different approaches, and never stop learning. The most rewarding levels are those that seamlessly blend challenge, exploration, and narrative into a cohesive and unforgettable experience.

5.3 Optimizing Performance in VR

Smooth frame rates and low latency are crucial for a comfortable and immersive VR experience. These factors directly impact presence, the feeling of "being there" inside the virtual environment. A stuttering, laggy experience can quickly break that immersion and even lead to motion sickness. Optimizing performance, therefore, is paramount to enjoying VR to its fullest.

One of the most significant factors influencing VR performance is your computer's graphics card. Think of it as the engine that drives the visual experience. A powerful GPU can render complex scenes and high resolutions smoothly, while a weaker one will struggle, leading to dropped frames and a choppy image. Check the recommended specifications for your specific VR headset and games. Often, exceeding these recommendations, especially regarding the graphics card, significantly enhances the experience. It's a worthwhile investment if you're serious about VR.

Beyond the raw power of your GPU, your CPU also plays a critical role. The CPU manages the complex calculations and data flow required for VR, ensuring that the various components of the system work in harmony. While a high-end CPU isn't as crucial as a powerful GPU, a bottleneck here can still negatively impact performance. A balanced system, with a CPU capable of keeping up with the demands of the GPU and VR headset, is essential for optimal performance. Regularly check for driver updates for both your GPU and CPU, as these updates often include performance optimizations and bug fixes that can significantly improve your VR experience.

The software you run also impacts VR performance. Background applications consume system resources, competing with the VR software for processing power and memory. Close unnecessary programs before launching your VR experience. Consider using dedicated game optimization tools that can automatically manage background processes and allocate resources more efficiently to the VR application. This ensures that the

VR software has access to the maximum available resources, leading to smoother frame rates and reduced latency.

Physical environment setup plays a surprisingly important role. Ensure your VR playspace is free of obstacles and that your sensors are positioned correctly. Obstructed sensors can lead to tracking issues, which can manifest as jerky movements or a loss of positional awareness within the virtual environment. Consult the setup guide for your specific VR system for optimal sensor placement. Different headsets have different requirements, and proper setup is crucial for a seamless experience. Experiment with different sensor placements to find what works best in your specific environment.

Cable management is often overlooked but can significantly impact your VR experience. Tangled or strained cables can restrict your movement and even cause disconnections, disrupting immersion. Use cable management solutions like ceiling pulleys or retractable cable reels to keep your cables organized and out of the way. This allows for greater freedom of movement within your playspace and reduces the risk of accidental disconnections. A clean and organized playspace contributes not only to better performance but also to safety and comfort during your VR sessions.

VR settings within applications themselves offer further avenues for optimization. Adjusting graphical settings, such as resolution and texture quality, can dramatically impact performance. Lowering these settings reduces the workload on your GPU, allowing for smoother frame rates.

Experiment with different settings to find the optimal balance between visual fidelity and performance. Many VR games offer detailed graphical settings menus, allowing you to fine-tune the experience to match your hardware capabilities.

Consider the specific requirements of each application. Some VR experiences are more demanding than others. For graphically intensive applications, lower settings may be necessary to achieve a comfortable frame rate. For less demanding experiences, you can push the settings higher for enhanced visual quality. Understanding the relationship between graphical settings and performance is crucial for optimizing your VR experience.

Beyond graphical settings, some VR applications offer additional performance optimization options. These might include features like asynchronous reprojection or interleaved reprojection. These techniques can help maintain a smooth frame rate even when the system is struggling to keep up with the demands of the virtual environment. Familiarize yourself with the specific performance options available in each application you use.

The temperature of your components also plays a role, albeit often subtle. Overheating can lead to performance throttling, where the system reduces performance to prevent damage. Ensure adequate cooling for your system, especially the GPU. Consider using additional fans or even liquid cooling solutions to keep temperatures under control. Monitoring your system temperatures during VR sessions can help identify potential overheating issues.

Regular maintenance of your system is also essential. Dust buildup can hinder airflow and contribute to overheating. Periodically clean your computer's internal components, including the fans and heatsinks. This ensures that your system can operate at its optimal performance level.

Finally, keep your VR software and drivers up to date. Developers frequently release updates that include performance improvements and bug fixes. Staying up to date with these updates ensures you're taking advantage of the latest optimizations and fixes. Check for updates regularly, both for your VR headset's software and for the individual VR applications you use. By following these tips, you can significantly enhance your VR experience.

5.4 Creating Believable Worlds

A vibrant, believable world draws readers in and doesn't let go. It becomes a character in its own right, shaping the narrative and influencing the actions of those within it. Building such a world requires more than just a cool setting; it demands careful consideration of the intricate details that breathe life into a fictional space. Think beyond the superficial—consider the rules, the culture, the very air your characters breathe.

One of the most critical aspects of world-building is establishing consistent internal logic. This forms the bedrock upon which all other elements rest. Your world doesn't need to mirror our own, but it does need to make sense within its own framework. Magic systems, technological advancements, societal structures—all must adhere to a set of defined principles. If dragons exist, what are their limitations? If your society is built on advanced technology, where does its energy come from? By answering these questions, you create a sense of order and predictability, even in the most fantastical settings. This allows your readers to suspend their disbelief and become truly immersed.

Cultural nuances add depth and richness to your world. Consider the traditions, rituals, and beliefs of your inhabitants. How do they celebrate? What are their taboos? How does their history shape their present? These details, seemingly small, add layers of complexity and contribute to a more authentic and engaging reading experience. A culture's relationship with its environment is equally crucial. Do they live in harmony with nature, or do they exploit it? How does the landscape impact their architecture, clothing, and cuisine? Exploring these connections creates a more holistic and believable world.

The environment itself plays a vital role. Go beyond simply describing a beautiful landscape. Consider the climate, the flora and fauna, the natural resources. How do these factors impact the lives of your characters? A desert society will have different concerns than a coastal community. A world rich in magical energy might have unique ecosystems and creatures. By meticulously crafting your environment, you add another layer of realism and depth to your narrative. Think about the smells, the sounds, the very texture of the world. These sensory details can transport your readers and make them feel truly present.

Don't neglect the political and economic systems that govern your world. Who holds power? How is wealth distributed? What are the major conflicts and tensions? These elements shape the social dynamics and create opportunities for conflict and intrigue. A rigidly hierarchical society will function differently from a democratic one. A world ravaged by scarcity will have different priorities than one of abundance. By carefully considering these structures, you add a layer of realism and complexity to your world.

Language is another powerful tool for world-building. While you don't need to create an entirely new language, incorporating unique phrases, slang, or dialects can add flavor and authenticity. Consider how different social groups might speak. Do they have distinct accents or vocabulary? How does language reflect their culture and history? Even subtle linguistic variations can enrich your world and make it feel more alive.

Remember that your world is not static. It evolves and changes over time, just like our own. Consider the history of your world. What major events have shaped its present? What are the ongoing conflicts and tensions? How is your world changing, and how do these changes affect your characters? By incorporating a sense of history and change, you create a dynamic and engaging setting that feels real.

Don't be afraid to break from traditional tropes and create something truly unique. Borrowing elements from existing worlds can be a good starting point, but don't be afraid to experiment and put your own spin on things. The most compelling worlds are often those that defy expectations and offer something new.

Finally, remember that world-building is an ongoing process. As you write, you'll discover new aspects of your world and refine your understanding of its intricacies. Don't be afraid to revise and expand upon your initial ideas as your story develops. The key is to stay curious and keep exploring.

Crafting a believable world requires patience, attention to detail, and a willingness to delve deep into the nuances of your creation. It's about more than just describing a setting; it's about building a living, breathing ecosystem that feels as real as our own. By considering these elements, you can create a world that will not only captivate your readers but also enrich your storytelling in profound ways. The reward is a richer, more immersive reading experience that will stay with your audience long after they've finished the last page. Embrace the challenge, and let your imagination soar.

5.5 Accessibility in VR Design

Consider the reach of your virtual world. Who might want to experience it, and what barriers might they face? Designing for accessibility isn't about ticking boxes; it's about opening doors to everyone. It's about fostering a truly inclusive environment where everyone feels welcome and can participate fully, regardless of their physical or cognitive abilities. This means thinking beyond the typical user and considering individuals with visual, auditory, motor, or cognitive impairments.

One crucial aspect is providing alternative navigation methods. While traditional VR relies heavily on hand controllers and physical movement, these can be challenging for users with limited mobility or dexterity. Implement options like teleportation, gaze-based navigation, and voice commands. These alternatives can significantly improve the experience for users with motor impairments, enabling them to navigate the virtual world with ease. Think about how someone using a wheelchair might navigate your VR space. Can they reach all the interactive elements? Are there clear pathways free from obstacles?

Visual accessibility is equally important. Many users experience low vision or color blindness, so ensure sufficient contrast between foreground and background elements. Offer customizable text sizes and fonts, and incorporate audio descriptions for key visuals. This not only benefits users with visual impairments but also enhances the experience for everyone in low-light environments. Imagine trying to navigate a dimly lit virtual room with small, low-contrast text. Frustrating, right? That's the reality for many users if visual accessibility isn't prioritized.

Auditory information is often crucial for immersion and understanding in VR. Provide captions and transcripts for all audio content, including dialogue, sound effects, and environmental sounds. This is vital for users with hearing impairments, but it also benefits those in noisy environments or those learning a new language. Consider spatial audio cues to help users locate the source of sounds, further enhancing immersion and accessibility. Think about a user who relies on audio cues to understand their surroundings. Without proper audio descriptions and captions, they might miss critical information or become disoriented.

Cognitive accessibility often gets overlooked, but it's just as important as physical accessibility. Provide clear and concise instructions, avoid overwhelming users with too much information at once, and offer tutorials or guided experiences. Allow users to adjust the pace of the experience and provide options to repeat instructions or tutorials. Consider incorporating visual aids and symbols to reinforce key information. Remember, a clear and intuitive interface is beneficial for everyone, not just those with cognitive impairments. Imagine a user with autism experiencing sensory overload in a cluttered and confusing virtual environment. By prioritizing cognitive accessibility, we can create more calming and manageable experiences.

Physical comfort is another crucial aspect of accessibility. VR sessions can sometimes be lengthy, so allow users to take breaks and adjust their physical position. Consider offering different comfort settings, such as adjustable seating or the ability to customize the virtual environment to reduce motion sickness. This not only benefits users with physical limitations but enhances the overall experience for everyone. Think about how tiring it can be to stand for extended periods in VR. Providing seating options and breaks can significantly improve user comfort and enjoyment. User testing is paramount. The best way to ensure your VR experience is truly accessible is to involve users with diverse abilities in the testing process. Gather feedback from users with visual, auditory, motor, and cognitive impairments. Their insights will be invaluable in identifying potential accessibility issues and refining your design. Remember, accessibility is not a one-size-fits-all solution; it's an ongoing process of learning and improvement. Consider forming a diverse accessibility testing group. Their direct feedback will be far more valuable than any assumptions you might make.

Don't think of accessibility as an added burden; view it as an opportunity to expand your audience and create a more inclusive and welcoming virtual world. By incorporating these accessibility features, you can make your VR experience enjoyable and engaging for everyone. This not only benefits users with disabilities but enhances the experience for all users. Imagine a world where everyone can participate in virtual reality, regardless of their abilities. That's the power of accessible design.

Remember, designing for accessibility is not just about compliance; it's about creating a truly inclusive experience. It's about making sure that everyone has the opportunity to explore, learn, and connect in the virtual world. This involves careful consideration of the user interface, interaction design, and overall user experience. By designing with accessibility in mind, you're not only creating a more inclusive experience, but also a better experience for everyone.

Finally, stay updated on the latest accessibility guidelines and best practices. Technology is constantly evolving, and so are accessibility standards. By staying informed, you can ensure your VR experiences remain accessible and inclusive for everyone. This includes staying abreast of new assistive technologies and incorporating them into your design whenever possible. By embracing a proactive approach to accessibility, you'll be well-equipped to create truly inclusive and enjoyable VR experiences for everyone.

6 The Future of Virtual Reality

The trajectory of virtual reality is not a straight line but rather an expanding web of interconnected advancements. We stand at a precipice, on the cusp of innovations that promise to fundamentally reshape how we interact with the digital realm and, by extension, the physical world. One key area of development lies in enhancing sensory feedback. Current VR experiences primarily engage sight and sound. However, the incorporation of haptic technology—the science of touch—is rapidly evolving. Imagine feeling the texture of a virtual object, the weight of a virtual tool, or the resistance of a virtual environment. This level of tactile feedback will significantly amplify the sense of presence and immersion, making virtual experiences feel tangibly real. The integration of advanced haptics will revolutionize fields like surgical training, industrial design, and even artistic expression, allowing for unprecedented levels of precision and control.

Beyond haptics, the evolution of display technology is poised to redefine visual fidelity in VR. Higher resolutions, wider fields of view, and improved refresh rates are already on the horizon. These advancements will minimize screen-door effects, reduce latency, and create visuals that are indistinguishable from reality. Furthermore, the emergence of foveated rendering—a technique that focuses processing power on the area where the user is looking—promises to dramatically enhance visual quality while optimizing performance. This technology allows for incredibly detailed environments without overwhelming the system's resources, paving the way for truly breathtaking virtual landscapes.

The convergence of VR with other emerging technologies like artificial intelligence and blockchain will unlock entirely new possibilities. Imagine personalized virtual environments that adapt to your preferences and learn from your behavior, offering curated experiences tailored to your individual needs. Blockchain technology could enable secure digital ownership of virtual assets, fostering new economies and creative opportunities within virtual worlds. The decentralized nature of blockchain also has the potential to create more democratic and user-driven VR platforms, where creators and users have greater control over their experiences and data.

The metaverse, a persistent shared virtual world, represents a significant evolutionary step for VR. This interconnected network of virtual spaces will allow users to seamlessly transition between different experiences, interact with others, and build communities. The metaverse holds immense potential for social interaction, entertainment, education, and even commerce. Imagine attending a virtual concert with friends from across the globe, collaborating on a design project in a shared virtual workspace, or exploring historical landmarks from the comfort of your home. The metaverse promises to blur the lines between the physical and digital, creating a hybrid reality that expands our social and experiential horizons.

However, the rapid advancement of VR also raises important ethical considerations. Issues of privacy, data security, accessibility, and potential psychological impacts must be addressed proactively. As we spend increasing amounts of time in virtual worlds, it is crucial to develop frameworks and guidelines that ensure responsible development and usage. Questions surrounding digital identity, ownership, and the potential for manipulation within virtual spaces require careful consideration. Open discussions and collaborative efforts between developers, policymakers, and users are essential to navigate these complex ethical challenges and ensure that the future of VR is both innovative and equitable.

The democratization of VR technology is another key aspect of its future. As hardware costs decrease and software becomes more accessible, VR will move beyond the realm of enthusiasts and early adopters and become a mainstream technology. This wider adoption will fuel further innovation and lead to a diversification of VR experiences, catering to a broader range of interests and needs. Imagine accessible VR tools for education, empowering students with immersive learning experiences across various subjects. Visualize therapists using VR to treat phobias and anxieties, providing patients with safe and controlled environments to confront their fears. Envision architects and designers collaborating in shared virtual spaces, refining building plans and product prototypes with unprecedented precision. The democratization of VR will unlock its transformative potential across numerous sectors, revolutionizing how we learn, work, and interact with the world around us. The convergence of these technological advancements, coupled with thoughtful ethical considerations and increased accessibility, paints a vibrant picture of the future of virtual reality – a future where the boundaries of the digital and physical worlds continue to blur, offering unprecedented opportunities for human connection, creativity, and exploration.

6.1 Emerging Technologies in VR

Extended reality (XR), encompassing virtual reality (VR), augmented reality (AR), and mixed reality (MR), is rapidly transforming how we interact with the digital world. VR, in particular, offers immersive experiences that transport users to entirely new environments, simulated or otherwise. This potential extends far beyond entertainment, impacting fields like healthcare, education, and engineering. As technology evolves, several key trends are shaping the future of VR.

Haptic feedback is crucial for enhancing realism within virtual environments. Early VR experiences relied heavily on visual and auditory stimulation. Now, sophisticated haptic devices are emerging, allowing users to "feel" virtual objects. These range from gloves and suits that provide pressure and temperature sensations to advanced systems that simulate textures and even impacts. This tactile dimension adds a layer of immersion, making virtual interactions more intuitive and engaging. Imagine a surgeon practicing a complex procedure in a VR simulation, feeling the resistance of virtual tissue, or an architect experiencing the texture of various building materials before construction begins.

Volumetric capture and display are pushing the boundaries of realism in VR. Traditional VR relies on computer-generated imagery (CGI) to create virtual worlds. However, volumetric capture allows for the creation of photorealistic representations of real people and objects. This technology uses multiple cameras to capture a subject from various angles, creating a 3D model that can be integrated into a VR environment. Paired with advanced display technologies that offer higher resolutions and wider fields of view, volumetric capture is enabling more lifelike and believable virtual experiences. This has significant implications for fields like telepresence and virtual production, blurring the lines between physical and digital realities.

Eye-tracking technology is enabling more natural and intuitive interactions in VR. By monitoring a user's eye movements, VR systems can determine where they are looking and adjust the virtual environment accordingly. This allows for features like foveated rendering, which optimizes the visual fidelity of the area the user is focusing on, improving performance and image quality. Eye tracking also enables more realistic avatars, allowing for nuanced expressions and non-verbal communication within virtual spaces. Moreover, it opens doors for research in fields like psychology and human-computer interaction, offering insights into how people perceive and navigate virtual environments.

Artificial intelligence (AI) is playing an increasingly important role in enhancing VR experiences. AI algorithms can be used to create more dynamic and responsive virtual worlds, populating them with intelligent agents that interact realistically with users. AI can also be used to personalize VR experiences, tailoring the environment and challenges to the individual user's preferences and skill level. Furthermore, AI-powered tools can streamline the creation of VR content, automating tasks like 3D modeling and animation. This democratizes access to VR development, enabling more creators to bring their visions to life.

5G and edge computing are transforming how VR content is delivered and experienced. The high bandwidth and low latency of 5G networks enable the streaming of high-quality VR experiences without the need for powerful local hardware. Edge computing, which distributes processing power closer to the user, further reduces latency and improves the responsiveness of VR applications. This opens up new possibilities for location-based VR entertainment and collaborative VR experiences. Imagine participating in a shared virtual workspace with colleagues from around the world, collaborating on a 3D design project in real-time, with no noticeable lag.

Brain-computer interfaces (BCIs) represent a cutting-edge area of research with the potential to revolutionize how we interact with VR. While still in its early stages, BCI technology allows for direct communication between the brain and a computer, bypassing traditional input devices like controllers or keyboards. In the context of VR, BCIs could enable users to control virtual objects with their thoughts, creating a truly immersive and intuitive experience. Imagine navigating a virtual world simply by thinking about where you want to go, or manipulating virtual objects with the power of your mind.

While these advancements promise exciting new possibilities, ethical considerations must be addressed as VR technology becomes more sophisticated and pervasive. Issues like privacy, data security, and the potential for addiction need to be carefully considered. Furthermore, the psychological impact of immersive VR experiences needs to be further studied to ensure the responsible development and deployment of this powerful technology. As we venture further into the virtual frontier, thoughtful consideration of these ethical implications is crucial for creating a positive and sustainable future for VR.

The future of VR is bright, driven by ongoing innovation in hardware, software, and supporting technologies. From enhanced haptic feedback to the potential of brain-computer interfaces, these emerging technologies are shaping a future where the lines between the physical and digital worlds become increasingly blurred. As VR continues to evolve, it promises to transform not only how we entertain ourselves, but also how we learn, work, and interact with the world around us. This evolution will demand careful consideration of the ethical implications, ensuring a future where VR benefits humanity as a whole. The journey into virtual reality is just beginning, and the potential for transformative experiences is vast.

6.2 The Metaverse and its Implications

The buzz around the metaverse is undeniable. From tech giants to gaming communities, everyone seems to be talking about it. But beyond the hype, what exactly is the metaverse, and how will it reshape our lives? The metaverse isn't a single place or platform. Think of it more as a convergence of technologies – virtual reality (VR), augmented reality (AR), and the internet – creating persistent, shared, 3D spaces where we can interact with each other and digital content in new and immersive ways. Imagine attending a concert with friends from across the globe, all from the comfort of your living room, or collaborating on a design project in a virtual office space, manipulating 3D models as if they were physically present. This is the promise of the metaverse.

One of the most significant implications of the metaverse is its potential to revolutionize social interaction. We're already seeing glimpses of this with virtual concerts and social VR platforms. These spaces offer opportunities to connect with people in ways that transcend geographical limitations, fostering a sense of community and shared experience. Imagine virtual book clubs where you can discuss literature with fellow enthusiasts in a simulated café, or attending a virtual cooking class with a renowned chef, interacting with them and other participants in real time. The possibilities for social connection are vast and constantly evolving.

Beyond social interaction, the metaverse also holds tremendous potential for education and training. Imagine learning history by stepping into a virtual recreation of ancient Rome, or mastering a complex surgical procedure through a VR simulation. These immersive experiences offer a level of engagement and interactivity that traditional learning methods simply can't match. Furthermore, the metaverse can democratize access to education, allowing individuals from underserved communities to participate in learning experiences that would otherwise be inaccessible. Students could attend virtual lectures by world-renowned professors or explore simulated environments that recreate historical events or scientific phenomena.

The metaverse is also poised to transform the world of work. Remote collaboration can become more seamless and engaging, with virtual offices allowing teams to work together in shared 3D spaces, regardless of their physical location. Imagine architects collaborating on a building design in a virtual environment, manipulating 3D models and making real-time changes together. Or consider customer service representatives assisting clients in a virtual store, providing personalized support and demonstrations. These applications demonstrate the power of the metaverse to enhance productivity and efficiency.

Of course, with any new technology, there are challenges and potential downsides to consider. One major concern is the issue of privacy and data security. As we spend more time in virtual environments, the amount of personal data collected will increase exponentially. Ensuring the responsible and ethical use of this data is crucial to prevent misuse and protect individual privacy. Strong regulations and transparent data practices will be essential to mitigate these risks.

Another challenge is the potential for digital divide. Access to the necessary technology and infrastructure, such as high-speed internet and VR headsets, may not be evenly distributed, creating disparities in access to the metaverse and its opportunities. Bridging this digital divide through initiatives that promote digital literacy and affordable access to technology will be vital to ensure that everyone can participate in the metaverse.

Accessibility is another crucial consideration. The metaverse must be designed to be inclusive and accessible to individuals with disabilities. This requires careful attention to interface design, user controls, and assistive technologies. Ensuring that the metaverse is accessible to everyone, regardless of their physical or cognitive abilities, is paramount.

The economic implications of the metaverse are also substantial. New industries and job markets will emerge, creating opportunities for developers, designers, content creators, and other professionals. The metaverse will also impact existing industries, transforming how businesses operate and interact with customers. Understanding these economic shifts and preparing for the evolving job market will be critical for individuals and organizations alike.

Furthermore, the metaverse raises important questions about identity and self-expression. In virtual environments, we can create avatars that represent different aspects of ourselves, or even entirely different personas. This opens up exciting possibilities for self-discovery and experimentation, but also raises ethical questions about authenticity and the blurring lines between the physical and virtual worlds. How will these evolving notions of identity impact our interactions and relationships, both online and offline? Finally, the metaverse has the potential to reshape our relationship with the physical world. As we spend more time in virtual environments, how will this impact our engagement with the real world? Will it lead to greater social isolation, or will it enhance our real-world connections by fostering a sense of community and shared experience? These are complex questions that require careful consideration as we navigate the evolving landscape of the metaverse. Understanding the implications of this transformative technology is essential for individuals, businesses, and policymakers alike. As we continue to explore the possibilities of the metaverse, it's crucial to approach this new frontier with a balanced perspective, acknowledging both its potential benefits and its potential risks.

6.3 Ethical Considerations in VR

Immersive technologies offer unprecedented opportunities for connection and experience. But with this power comes a new layer of ethical complexities, particularly pertinent to virtual reality. As we delve deeper into virtual worlds, we must grapple with the implications of our actions and designs on individual users and the broader societal landscape. The ethical considerations in VR are not mere abstract concepts; they are vital for shaping a future where this technology fosters positive growth and avoids potential harms.

One crucial area is the blurring of reality and virtuality. VR experiences can be incredibly visceral, evoking powerful emotional and psychological responses. This blurring of lines can have profound consequences for users, especially those susceptible to suggestibility or who struggle to differentiate between real and virtual experiences. Designers and developers must consider the potential for psychological distress, addiction, and dissociation. Building in mechanisms for regular breaks, clear delineations between the virtual and real world, and accessible support resources are essential first steps. Open and honest conversations about the limitations and potential risks of VR are equally crucial.

The concept of presence, the feeling of actually being within a virtual environment, raises further ethical concerns. As VR technology advances, the sense of presence becomes increasingly convincing. This enhanced realism can amplify the ethical weight of virtual actions. For example, acts of violence or harassment within a VR environment, even if lacking physical consequences, can carry significant emotional and psychological impact. Developing community standards, implementing effective moderation strategies, and fostering empathy within virtual spaces are crucial for mitigating these risks.

Furthermore, the collection and use of personal data in VR raise significant privacy concerns. VR headsets and related technologies often track extensive biometric and behavioral data, including eye movements, body language, and even emotional responses. This data trove can be invaluable for improving user experience and personalizing content, but it also presents a significant risk of misuse. Transparent data collection practices, robust security measures, and user control over their data are paramount. Users should have the right to know what data is being collected, how it will be used, and with whom it will be shared. They should also have the option to opt out of data collection or delete their data entirely.

Accessibility and inclusivity represent another key ethical dimension. The cost of VR equipment can create a digital divide, limiting access for individuals and communities with fewer resources. Furthermore, VR experiences may not be designed with accessibility in mind, excluding users with disabilities. A commitment to affordable VR options, inclusive design practices, and diverse representation within virtual worlds is essential for ensuring that this technology benefits everyone.

Beyond individual users, VR also has implications for society as a whole. The potential for virtual experiences to influence real-world beliefs and behaviors cannot be ignored. Consider the use of VR for training, education, and even political advocacy. Ensuring that these applications are used responsibly and ethically is of utmost importance. Transparency about the purpose and potential biases of VR experiences, coupled with critical thinking skills, can empower users to navigate virtual information landscapes effectively.

Another societal concern is the potential for VR to exacerbate existing inequalities. If access to VR technology and experiences is not distributed equitably, it could deepen social and economic disparities. Addressing these concerns requires a concerted effort from developers, policymakers, and educators to promote equitable access and responsible development. This includes investing in public access programs, supporting research on the societal impact of VR, and fostering dialogue on the ethical implications of this transformative technology.

The creation of virtual identities also presents ethical dilemmas. While the ability to craft and inhabit different personas in VR can be empowering and liberating, it can also lead to issues of authenticity, misrepresentation, and deception. Clear guidelines and community standards regarding the representation of identity in virtual spaces are needed to mitigate these risks.

Finally, the very nature of reality itself is being challenged by the rise of immersive technologies. As VR becomes more sophisticated and integrated into our lives, the line between the physical and virtual worlds will continue to blur. This blurring presents profound philosophical questions about the nature of experience, consciousness, and even what it means to be human. Engaging in open and thoughtful discussions about these questions is vital for navigating the future of VR and its impact on our understanding of reality.

Consider the long-term implications of these ethical considerations. The choices we make today will shape the future of VR and its impact on individuals and society. By prioritizing ethical design, responsible development, and open dialogue, we can harness the transformative power of VR for good, creating a future where this technology enhances human connection, fosters empathy, and expands the boundaries of human experience. This requires continuous reflection, adaptation, and a commitment to putting human well-being at the forefront of technological advancement.

7 VR Beyond Entertainment

Immersive learning environments are rapidly transforming education and training. Imagine a medical student practicing a complex surgical procedure without risk to a patient, or a firefighter navigating a burning building in a safe, simulated environment. This is the power of VR in education. It offers experiential learning that transcends traditional methods, providing a level of engagement and knowledge retention that textbooks and lectures simply can't match. From dissecting virtual organs to exploring ancient civilizations, VR opens up a world of possibilities for interactive and personalized learning experiences tailored to individual needs. The ability to repeat scenarios, receive immediate feedback, and learn from mistakes in a consequence-free environment makes VR an invaluable tool for skill development across various disciplines.

VR's therapeutic applications are equally profound. Exposure therapy, a common treatment for phobias and anxiety disorders, has been significantly enhanced by VR. By creating controlled, virtual environments, therapists can guide patients through gradual exposure to their fears, helping them manage anxiety and develop coping mechanisms. For instance, someone with a fear of public speaking can practice presenting to a virtual audience, building confidence and reducing anxiety in a safe and supportive setting. Furthermore, VR is being used to treat post-traumatic stress disorder (PTSD), providing a platform for patients to revisit traumatic experiences in a controlled therapeutic environment. The immersive nature of VR allows for a deeper level of emotional processing and healing, offering new hope for individuals struggling with mental health challenges.

Beyond education and therapy, VR is revolutionizing business and industry. Architectural firms use VR to create immersive walkthroughs of building designs, allowing clients to experience the space before construction even begins. Manufacturing companies employ VR for training purposes, simulating complex assembly processes and allowing employees to practice without the risk of damaging expensive equipment or injuring themselves. Even the automotive industry utilizes VR for design and prototyping, allowing engineers to visualize and refine vehicle designs in a virtual environment. This reduces development costs and accelerates the design process. These are just a few examples of how VR is transforming various industries, enhancing efficiency, and driving innovation.

The potential applications of VR are continuously expanding. From virtual tourism experiences that allow users to explore far-off destinations from the comfort of their homes to immersive art installations that redefine creative expression, VR is pushing the boundaries of what's possible.

Consider the potential for virtual archaeological digs, allowing researchers to explore ancient sites without disturbing delicate artifacts, or virtual field trips for students to experience ecosystems around the world. The ability to connect with others in shared virtual spaces opens doors for new forms of social interaction and collaboration, transcending geographical boundaries and fostering a sense of global community. The expanding horizon of VR promises a future where the boundaries of reality are constantly being redefined.

The impact of virtual reality on society is far-reaching and transformative. As VR becomes more accessible and integrated into our daily lives, it will inevitably shape the way we learn, work, interact, and experience the world around us. This presents both exciting opportunities and important considerations. We must consider the ethical implications of VR, addressing issues such as privacy, accessibility, and the potential for misuse. Furthermore, as with any technological advancement, it's crucial to ensure equitable access to VR technology and address the potential for a digital divide. By fostering thoughtful dialogue and responsible development, we can harness the power of VR to create a more enriching and equitable future for all. The ongoing evolution of VR requires continuous exploration and careful consideration of its societal impact. By embracing a collaborative and ethical approach, we can navigate the complexities of this transformative technology and unlock its full potential for positive change. This ongoing conversation and adaptation are crucial as we navigate the evolving landscape of virtual reality and its integration into our lives.

7.1 VR in Education and Training

Immersive learning experiences offer a unique advantage in education and training. Virtual Reality (VR) provides an engaging environment where individuals can interact with simulated scenarios, fostering deeper understanding and skill development. From exploring ancient ruins to dissecting a human heart without the ethical and logistical constraints of the real world, VR opens doors to possibilities previously confined to textbooks and lectures. This transformative technology holds the potential to revolutionize how we learn and train across diverse fields.
Consider medical students learning complex surgical procedures. Traditionally, they observe seasoned surgeons and practice on cadavers or synthetic models. VR introduces a dynamic alternative. Students can now step into a virtual operating room, equipped with virtual instruments, and perform simulated surgeries with haptic feedback. This allows for repeated practice without risk to patients and provides instant feedback on their technique, accelerating the learning curve and boosting confidence. Such risk-free environments are invaluable for honing skills that demand precision and accuracy. Imagine a pilot training in a flight simulator, a firefighter navigating a burning building, or a surgeon performing a delicate procedure – all within the safe confines of a virtual world.

The benefits extend beyond procedural training. VR can create compelling simulations of historical events, geographical locations, or even abstract concepts. History students can walk through the streets of ancient Rome, geography students can explore the Amazon rainforest, and chemistry students can manipulate molecules in three-dimensional space. These immersive experiences foster a deeper understanding of the subject matter by engaging multiple senses and encouraging active participation, unlike passive learning methods. Students aren't just reading about history; they are experiencing it. They are not just memorizing facts; they are building knowledge through interaction and exploration.

Accessibility is another key advantage of VR in education and training. VR can overcome geographical barriers, bringing world-class learning experiences to remote or underserved communities. Imagine students in a rural village accessing a virtual library filled with interactive learning materials or participating in a virtual field trip to a world-renowned museum. Such opportunities level the playing field and provide equal access to quality education, regardless of location. The ability to customize the learning pace and provide individualized feedback further enhances accessibility for learners with diverse needs and learning styles.

The cost-effectiveness of VR is increasingly compelling. While the initial investment in VR equipment might seem significant, the long-term benefits can outweigh the costs. For instance, training programs that rely on expensive physical resources, like flight simulators or specialized lab equipment, can find a more affordable and scalable solution in VR. Moreover, the ability to repeat training scenarios indefinitely without consuming physical resources translates to significant cost savings over time. Consider the cost of repeatedly building and dismantling a physical set for disaster response training compared to the cost of running a VR simulation.

Beyond direct cost savings, VR can also reduce indirect costs associated with traditional training methods. Travel expenses, accommodation, and lost productivity due to time spent away from work can be minimized by conducting training in a virtual environment. This is particularly relevant for organizations with geographically dispersed teams or individuals requiring specialized training. Imagine the efficiency of training employees across multiple locations simultaneously, without the logistical complexities and expenses of bringing everyone together physically.

The integration of VR into existing educational frameworks requires careful planning and execution. Educators and trainers must develop clear learning objectives and design VR experiences that align with these objectives. Simply incorporating VR for the sake of novelty is insufficient. The technology should be used strategically to enhance learning outcomes and address specific pedagogical needs. A thoughtfully designed VR experience should be interactive, engaging, and relevant to the curriculum.

Effective implementation of VR in education requires addressing various challenges. Ensuring accessibility for all learners, including those with disabilities, is paramount. Developing high-quality VR content that is aligned with curriculum standards requires significant investment and expertise. Educators also need professional development opportunities to effectively integrate VR into their teaching practices. Ongoing research and evaluation are crucial to understand the long-term impact of VR on learning outcomes and identify best practices for implementation.

Teacher training and support are crucial for successful VR integration. Teachers need to understand how to effectively utilize VR technology in their classrooms and design engaging learning experiences. Professional development programs can equip teachers with the necessary skills and knowledge to leverage the potential of VR. Ongoing support and mentorship are essential to ensure that teachers feel comfortable and confident using VR as a teaching tool. This includes providing technical assistance, access to resources, and opportunities for collaboration and sharing best practices.

Looking ahead, advancements in VR technology promise even more immersive and personalized learning experiences. Haptic feedback, eye-tracking, and advanced graphics will enhance the realism and interactivity of VR simulations. Artificial intelligence can be leveraged to personalize learning pathways and provide tailored feedback to individual learners. The convergence of these technologies will create powerful learning environments that cater to diverse learning styles and optimize learning outcomes. As VR technology continues to evolve, its potential to transform education and training will only continue to grow. The future of learning is immersive, interactive, and personalized.

7.2 Therapeutic Applications of VR

Immersive virtual reality experiences offer a unique opportunity to address a range of psychological challenges. Unlike traditional therapeutic methods, VR allows for controlled, repeatable exposure to anxiety-provoking stimuli within a safe environment. This controlled exposure forms the foundation of many VR therapy applications, allowing individuals to confront their fears gradually and at their own pace. Imagine a fear of public speaking. Instead of facing a real audience immediately, a person can practice giving a presentation in a virtual auditorium, adjusting the size and responsiveness of the virtual crowd as their confidence grows.

The applications extend beyond simple phobias. Consider post-traumatic stress disorder (PTSD). VR can recreate traumatic scenarios in a safe and controlled manner, helping individuals process their experiences and reduce the intensity of their emotional responses. This allows for a form of exposure therapy that wouldn't be possible or ethical in the real world. For instance, a veteran struggling with memories of combat can revisit a virtual representation of a similar environment, gradually desensitizing themselves to the triggers that provoke anxiety and flashbacks. The therapist, meanwhile, can monitor their progress and adjust the experience as needed, ensuring the process remains therapeutic and doesn't re-traumatize the individual.

Beyond exposure therapy, VR offers exciting possibilities for skill development and cognitive rehabilitation. Individuals with autism spectrum disorder can practice social interaction skills in virtual environments, navigating scenarios like job interviews or social gatherings without the pressure of real-world consequences. This allows for repeated practice and the development of coping mechanisms for potentially stressful situations. Similarly, stroke survivors can utilize VR to regain lost motor skills through engaging and repetitive exercises, such as reaching for virtual objects or navigating virtual mazes. This gamified approach to rehabilitation can be more motivating than traditional methods, encouraging patients to actively participate in their recovery.

The potential of VR extends to pain management as well. Immersing patients in engaging virtual environments can distract them from chronic pain, reducing their reliance on medication. The immersive nature of VR helps shift the focus away from physical discomfort, offering a sense of escape and relaxation. Imagine a burn victim undergoing painful wound care. VR can transport them to a tranquil virtual landscape, minimizing their perception of pain and making the procedure more bearable. Studies have shown that VR can be particularly effective in managing phantom limb pain, providing a virtual representation of the missing limb and allowing patients to regain a sense of control over their sensations.

Moreover, VR offers a powerful tool for treating addiction. By simulating craving-inducing scenarios, VR allows individuals to practice coping mechanisms and relapse prevention strategies in a controlled environment. Someone struggling with alcohol addiction, for example, can be exposed to a virtual bar scene, learning to navigate the social pressures and triggers that might lead to relapse. This simulated exposure helps build resilience and equips them with the tools they need to manage real-world challenges. The interactive nature of VR allows for personalized scenarios tailored to the individual's specific triggers and vulnerabilities.

The accessibility of VR technology is also rapidly increasing. While the initial cost of VR headsets can be a barrier, the prices are steadily decreasing, and more affordable options are becoming available. Furthermore, the development of standalone VR headsets eliminates the need for expensive computers, making the technology more accessible to a wider range of users. This increased accessibility makes VR a promising tool for delivering mental health services to underserved populations, particularly those in rural areas with limited access to specialized care. Imagine a therapist being able to conduct virtual sessions with patients in remote locations, providing much-needed support without the logistical and financial barriers of traditional in-person therapy.

Furthermore, VR offers advantages in terms of data collection and treatment personalization. The highly controlled nature of virtual environments allows therapists to gather precise data on patient responses, tracking their progress and adjusting treatment plans accordingly. This data-driven approach can lead to more effective and personalized interventions.

For instance, in exposure therapy, therapists can monitor physiological responses like heart rate and skin conductance, tailoring the intensity of the virtual stimuli to ensure optimal therapeutic benefit. This level of personalization is difficult to achieve with traditional methods.

Ethical considerations are paramount in the therapeutic application of VR. Patient privacy and data security must be carefully protected. Clear guidelines and protocols are essential to ensure responsible and ethical use of this technology. Furthermore, it's crucial to address potential side effects, such as motion sickness or cyber sickness, and to carefully screen patients for suitability. Proper training and supervision of therapists are also essential to ensure the effective and ethical delivery of VR-based interventions. The long-term effects of VR therapy are still being studied, and ongoing research is essential to further refine and optimize its application.

While VR holds immense promise for transforming mental healthcare, it's important to remember that it's not a panacea. It's a tool that should be integrated into a comprehensive treatment plan, complementing traditional therapeutic approaches. The human element of therapy remains crucial, and VR should not be seen as a replacement for the therapeutic relationship. Rather, it's a powerful adjunct that can enhance the effectiveness of therapy and expand access to care. As the technology continues to evolve and research continues to accumulate, we can expect to see even more innovative and impactful applications of VR in the field of mental health.

The integration of VR into therapeutic practice represents a significant advancement in mental healthcare. By providing immersive and interactive experiences, VR offers unique opportunities to address a wide range of psychological challenges. From treating phobias and PTSD to managing pain and addiction, VR is empowering individuals to overcome their limitations and improve their quality of life. As we continue to explore the potential of this transformative technology, we can anticipate a future where VR plays an increasingly important role in promoting mental well-being.

7.3 VR for Business and Industry

The transformative potential of Virtual Reality (VR) is rapidly reshaping industries, offering unprecedented opportunities for innovation and efficiency. From streamlining design processes to enhancing employee training and revolutionizing customer engagement, VR is no longer a futuristic concept, but a tangible tool with real-world applications. Understanding its diverse capabilities is crucial for businesses seeking to leverage this cutting-edge technology.

One of the most compelling uses of VR lies in product design and prototyping. Imagine architects walking through a virtual building before a single brick is laid, or automotive engineers meticulously inspecting a car's internal workings without physical disassembly. This virtual exploration allows for early identification and correction of design flaws, saving significant time and resources. Modifications can be made in real-time within the virtual environment, fostering collaborative design and iterative improvements. This translates to faster development cycles, reduced prototyping costs, and ultimately, superior products.

VR's immersive nature also makes it a powerful tool for training and development. Traditional training methods often fall short in providing realistic, hands-on experience. VR, on the other hand, can simulate complex scenarios and environments, allowing employees to acquire practical skills in a safe and controlled setting. A surgeon can practice a delicate procedure countless times within a virtual operating room, a pilot can navigate challenging flight conditions in a virtual cockpit, and a maintenance technician can troubleshoot equipment malfunctions in a virtual factory. This experiential learning accelerates skill development, boosts confidence, and ultimately improves job performance.

Beyond internal operations, VR is transforming how businesses interact with customers. Imagine a retail store where customers can virtually try on clothes or visualize furniture in their homes before making a purchase. Or consider a travel agency offering immersive virtual tours of destinations, allowing clients to experience the sights and sounds of a place before booking their trip. These engaging experiences enhance customer satisfaction, drive sales conversions, and foster stronger brand loyalty. Moreover, VR provides valuable data on customer behavior and preferences, offering insights that can inform product development and marketing strategies.

The applications of VR in the healthcare industry are particularly noteworthy. From pain management and rehabilitation to surgical training and patient education, VR is revolutionizing medical practices. Patients undergoing physical therapy can engage in immersive exercises within virtual environments, while surgeons can practice complex procedures with unparalleled precision. VR also offers a powerful tool for mental health treatment, allowing therapists to create customized virtual scenarios for patients struggling with anxiety, phobias, and PTSD. This innovative application of VR is transforming patient care and improving health outcomes. Manufacturing and engineering industries are also experiencing significant benefits from VR adoption. Virtual factory tours allow engineers to identify potential bottlenecks in production lines and optimize workflows. Maintenance technicians can train on complex equipment in a safe environment, reducing the risk of accidents and improving repair efficiency. VR also facilitates remote collaboration, allowing engineers and technicians from different locations to work together on projects in a shared virtual space. This enhances communication, streamlines operations, and drives innovation within industrial settings.

While the benefits of VR are undeniable, successful implementation requires careful planning and consideration. Identifying specific business needs and objectives is paramount. Choosing the right hardware and software solutions is equally crucial. Investing in high-quality VR headsets and developing tailored applications that align with specific business goals ensures optimal performance and return on investment. Furthermore, user training and support are essential for successful VR adoption.

Employees need to be comfortable using the technology and understand its potential applications. Providing adequate training and ongoing support maximizes the effectiveness of VR implementation.

As VR technology continues to evolve, its applications will only expand. Businesses that embrace this transformative technology will gain a competitive edge in the marketplace. From enhanced customer experiences to improved operational efficiency and accelerated innovation, the potential benefits of VR are vast and far-reaching. Embracing this technology is no longer a question of "if," but "when." By strategically implementing VR solutions, businesses can unlock new levels of productivity, creativity, and growth. The future of business is immersive, and VR is leading the way.

The integration of VR with other emerging technologies, such as augmented reality (AR) and artificial intelligence, will further amplify its transformative potential. Imagine a factory floor where technicians use AR overlays to visualize equipment schematics while simultaneously receiving real-time performance data through AI-powered analytics. Or consider a retail environment where customers can interact with virtual product demonstrations while receiving personalized recommendations based on their past purchase history. These integrated solutions offer unprecedented opportunities for businesses to optimize operations, enhance customer engagement, and drive innovation across various industries.

Looking ahead, the widespread adoption of VR will necessitate the development of robust ecosystems and standardized platforms. Interoperability between different VR systems and devices will be crucial for seamless collaboration and data sharing. The creation of industry-specific VR applications and training programs will also be essential for maximizing the technology's potential. As the VR landscape matures, businesses will need to stay abreast of the latest advancements and adapt their strategies accordingly. Embracing a culture of experimentation and continuous learning will be key to harnessing the full power of VR and transforming business operations for the future.

7.4 The Expanding Horizon of VR

Immersive technologies are no longer a futuristic fantasy. They are rapidly transforming how we interact with the digital world, and virtual reality (VR) stands at the forefront of this revolution. From gaming and entertainment to education and healthcare, VR's potential seems limitless. Its capacity to transport us to other realms, to simulate experiences, and to connect us in novel ways is reshaping our understanding of what's possible. This evolution isn't just about better graphics or faster processors. It represents a fundamental shift in how we perceive and engage with information, experiences, and each other.

The accessibility of VR is a key driver of its expanding horizon. Once relegated to expensive, specialized equipment, VR headsets are now available at a range of price points, making the technology more accessible to the average consumer. This democratization has fueled a surge in creativity and innovation, with developers constantly pushing the boundaries of what VR can achieve. The increasing affordability of powerful computers also contributes to this growth, enabling more complex and immersive experiences. We're seeing a virtuous cycle where greater accessibility fosters wider adoption, which in turn encourages further development and refinement of the technology.

Beyond gaming, where VR initially gained traction, we're witnessing its integration into various sectors. In healthcare, VR is used for surgical training, pain management, and rehabilitation. Imagine a surgeon practicing a complex procedure in a virtual operating room, honing their skills without risk to a patient. Or consider a burn victim finding solace and pain relief in a virtual snowy landscape. These applications demonstrate VR's potential to revolutionize healthcare delivery and improve patient outcomes. The ability to create realistic simulations opens doors to new training methods and therapeutic interventions.

Education is another field ripe for transformation through VR. Students can explore ancient ruins, dissect a virtual frog, or travel through the human circulatory system, all from the comfort of their classroom. These immersive experiences can foster deeper understanding and engagement with learning materials, making education more interactive and memorable. By transcending the limitations of traditional textbooks and lectures, VR empowers educators to create dynamic and engaging learning environments. Think of the possibilities for students to collaborate on projects in shared virtual spaces, regardless of their physical location.

The business world is also embracing VR. Companies are using VR for employee training, product design, and virtual meetings. Imagine architects walking clients through a virtual model of a building before construction even begins, or engineers collaborating on a complex design in a shared virtual space. VR can streamline processes, improve communication, and foster innovation across diverse industries. The ability to visualize data and interact with virtual prototypes can significantly accelerate product development cycles.

Looking towards the future, the convergence of VR with other technologies like augmented reality (AR) and artificial intelligence promises even more transformative applications. Imagine a world where virtual and real-world elements seamlessly blend, creating hybrid experiences that enhance our perception and interaction with our surroundings. This convergence has the potential to reshape our relationship with technology in profound ways. Consider the possibilities for personalized learning experiences, tailored to individual student needs and learning styles.

The development of haptic feedback technology further enhances the immersive potential of VR. Haptic devices allow users to "feel" virtual objects, adding a crucial layer of realism to the experience. Imagine a surgeon feeling the resistance of virtual tissue during a simulated surgery, or a gamer experiencing the impact of a virtual weapon. These advancements blur the lines between the physical and digital worlds, creating more engaging and impactful experiences.

Social interaction within VR is another area of rapid evolution. Virtual worlds and social platforms are emerging, allowing users to connect and interact with each other in shared virtual spaces. Imagine attending a virtual concert with friends from across the globe, or collaborating on a creative project in a virtual studio. These social VR experiences are transforming the way we connect and communicate, breaking down geographical barriers and fostering new forms of community.

The ethical considerations surrounding VR are also gaining prominence. As the technology becomes more sophisticated and integrated into our lives, questions about privacy, security, and the potential for manipulation need careful consideration. It's crucial to develop ethical guidelines and regulations that ensure responsible development and deployment of VR technology. We must proactively address potential risks and ensure that VR benefits society as a whole.

The expanding horizon of VR represents a paradigm shift in how we interact with technology and the world around us. From entertainment and education to healthcare and business, VR is transforming industries and shaping the future of human experience. As the technology continues to evolve, its potential seems limitless, promising to create a world where the boundaries between the physical and digital realms become increasingly blurred. The journey into this immersive future is just beginning, and its impact on our lives will be profound.

7.5 Virtual Reality and Society

Immersive technologies, like virtual reality (VR), are no longer confined to the realm of science fiction. They are rapidly becoming integrated into our daily lives, impacting how we interact with each other, consume information, and even perceive reality itself. This integration presents a unique set of societal challenges and opportunities that we must carefully consider as we navigate this new technological landscape. The potential for both positive and negative consequences is significant, demanding a thoughtful and proactive approach to harnessing the power of VR for the betterment of society.

One of the most prominent areas where VR is making an impact is in social interaction. Platforms are emerging that allow individuals to connect with each other in virtual environments, transcending geographical limitations and fostering new forms of community. These virtual spaces offer opportunities for shared experiences, collaborative work, and even the formation of meaningful relationships. However, concerns remain about the potential for these virtual interactions to replace or diminish the value of real-world connections. Maintaining a healthy balance between the virtual and physical realms will be crucial for fostering well-rounded social development. It's vital to acknowledge the potential for both positive and negative consequences as we navigate this evolving social landscape.

Education is another sector poised for transformation through VR. Imagine students exploring ancient Rome, dissecting a human heart in 3D, or experiencing scientific concepts firsthand in immersive simulations. These possibilities have the potential to revolutionize the way we learn, making education more engaging, interactive, and accessible to a wider range of learners. Furthermore, VR can create personalized learning experiences tailored to individual student needs and learning styles. This individualized approach could address the limitations of traditional classroom settings, offering customized pathways to knowledge and skill development. As with social interaction, a balanced approach is key, ensuring that these technological advancements complement, rather than replace, the essential role of human educators in guiding and mentoring students.

The healthcare industry is also experiencing the transformative potential of VR. From pain management and rehabilitation to surgical training and mental health therapy, VR offers innovative solutions to complex medical challenges. For example, patients undergoing painful procedures can use VR to distract themselves and manage their discomfort. Physical therapists can utilize VR to create engaging rehabilitation exercises that motivate patients and track their progress. The potential applications are vast and continually expanding, offering exciting possibilities for improving patient care and advancing medical practices. Careful consideration of ethical implications and data privacy is crucial as we integrate these technologies into healthcare settings.

The entertainment industry, of course, has been an early adopter of VR technology. From immersive gaming experiences to interactive storytelling and virtual concerts, VR is reshaping how we consume and engage with entertainment. This shift opens up exciting new avenues for creativity and artistic expression, blurring the lines between the real and the virtual. However, the potential for addiction and escapism should be addressed proactively to ensure responsible usage and minimize potential negative consequences. Encouraging a healthy balance between virtual entertainment and real-world activities is essential for maintaining overall well-being.

Beyond these specific sectors, VR also has broader implications for society. It raises questions about identity, privacy, accessibility, and even the very nature of reality. As we spend more time in virtual environments, our sense of self and our interactions with others may be fundamentally altered. The lines between the physical and virtual worlds are blurring, creating a complex interplay of real and simulated experiences. Navigating this evolving landscape requires careful consideration of the ethical, social, and philosophical implications of these technologies.

Moreover, the accessibility of VR technology is a critical issue that must be addressed to ensure equitable access and avoid exacerbating existing inequalities. The cost of VR equipment and the digital literacy required to navigate these technologies can create barriers for marginalized communities. Efforts must be made to bridge this digital divide and ensure that the benefits of VR are accessible to all members of society, regardless of their socioeconomic status or technological proficiency. Promoting digital literacy and providing affordable access to VR technology are crucial steps in fostering a more inclusive and equitable future.

Furthermore, the potential for misuse of VR technology should not be overlooked. Concerns about privacy violations, manipulation, and the creation of realistic simulations that could be used for nefarious purposes must be carefully considered. Developing robust ethical guidelines and regulatory frameworks is essential for mitigating these risks and ensuring that VR is used responsibly and for the benefit of humanity. Open discussions and collaborative efforts among policymakers, technology developers, and the public are crucial for navigating these complex challenges.

Finally, the impact of VR on our perception of reality is a profound question that warrants ongoing exploration. As virtual experiences become increasingly immersive and indistinguishable from real-world sensations, the lines between what is real and what is simulated may become increasingly blurred. This blurring of boundaries raises fundamental questions about our understanding of reality, consciousness, and the nature of human experience. Exploring these philosophical implications is crucial for understanding the long-term impact of VR on our individual and collective consciousness.

In conclusion, VR is a transformative technology with the potential to reshape society in profound ways. By carefully considering the ethical, social, and practical implications of VR, we can harness its power for good and create a future where this technology enhances human lives and fosters a more connected, equitable, and informed world. This requires ongoing dialogue, collaboration, and a commitment to responsible innovation as we navigate the evolving landscape of virtual reality and its impact on society.

www.ingramcontent.com/pod-product-compliance
Lightning Source LLC
LaVergne TN
LVHW022225200926
848481LV00006B/2130
* 9 7 9 8 3 4 8 3 3 3 5 9 1 *